Insights of a Modern Mystic

A Day-by-Day Book of Uncommon Wisdom

MICHAEL J. ROADS

(6°)

SIX DEGREES PUBLISHING GROUP
PORTLAND OREGON USA

INSIGHTS OF A MODERN MYSTIC
A Day-by-Day Book of Uncommon Wisdom

Copyright © 2015 by Michael J. Roads

FIRST SIX DEGREES PUBLISHING GROUP SOFTCOVER EDITION
November 2015

ISBN: 978-1-942497-12-7
EBook ISBN: 978-1-942497-15-8

Six Degrees Publishing Group
5331 S. W. Macadam Avenue, Suite 258
Portland, OR 97239

Published previously under ISBN number 9780975847602
The Oracle © 2005 Roadslight Pty. Limited

Published in the U.S.A.

1 3 7 9 10 8 6 4 2

This day-by-day book is dedicated to the Truth that resides in every human Being.

Introduction

I am a modern mystic. This book is based on my meta-physical travels, my enlightened experience of life, and a broader, far more profound perspective than comes from everyday living. And yet, it is in everyday living that my insights are so applicable.

This book offers insights into day-by-day life. I am offering a simple, occasionally ambiguous, yet always thought-provoking look at life. It is obvious that I am a lover of aphorisms! In this book, all the aphorisms come from me. An aphorism is a short pithy wisdom, expressing a Truth. I have deliberately written Truth with a capital T, for truth as it is expressed today often holds no Truth at all. Let me define it this way: truth today is casual, a point of view, depending on how you perceive it. If you view our planet from the eyes of a high-flying eagle, you see a very different reality than if viewed from the eyes of an earth-bound mouse. If you were asked to judge whose vision is the truth, you realise that truth is not relevant, it is all about perspective.

What are my credentials? I use Truth in this book from the overview of a spiritually and holistically enlightened man, seeing life from a holistic viewpoint. There is no possible comparison between the experience of Truth, and having a concept of it. The sum of 'bits of truth' do not add up to Truth, for Truth has never been fragmented. Truth is whole, constantly expanding in the unfolding moment of life.

Truth is not limited to a three-dimensional reality, nor is it contained by linear time, so when I write of Truth in this book, you may need to expand your vision. If you have a concept of Truth, then live the concept. Either it will take you to the portal of Truth, or it will reveal to you that the concept was based in falsity. There is a timing to Truth, and by living the concept you will precipitate the timing. Truth, however, is not intellectual, so the paradox is that although Truth can be recognised by the intellect, the intellect is unable to experience Truth. And Truth is an experience.

When I write 'self' in these pages, I refer to the identity self, whereas when I write 'Self' I refer to the spiritual 'Who I Am' Self. Equally with the word Love. When I capitalise Love, it indicates unconditional Love, or divine Love, or absolute Love, as opposed to "I love my new car!"

As you go through this book you will find that often I have repeated a particular theme, or I have reiterated it from several different viewpoints. This is deliberate. Some of the aphorisms look at the same theme from different angles, each designed to strongly imprint that particular insight into your consciousness. Some of the aphorisms follow a theme for a few days consecutively, while others are more random. If you find that you are strongly resisting a certain wisdom, then you can be sure that it's truth is knocking on the door of your subconscious resistance.

This is not a book to be read at a sitting. As a day-by-day book, it is an inspirational, even catalytic book, with the intention of drawing you, the reader, into a deeper experience of life. It is my intent to open you in a subtle and caring way, thereby creating less resistance from your subconscious program of self-denial.

You will find that I often write about your movie of Life. This movie is about the 'Continuity of Self.' Each frame of the movie is what we term a lifetime, and there are *very* many frames. Identity-self sees life as a single frame of the movie, whereas the Self you are relates to the whole movie as life; your life. This is the greater holistic viewpoint. The illusions of life are created by believing that a single linear time-frame is all life. In a greater reality the movie, 'The Continuity of Self' is holistic, meaning, your whole life - past and future - is expressing in this moment . . . now!

Before you begin, let me draw your attention to one particular statement I have made often in this book. Anything that you want to change, anything that offers value to your life, has to be *lived* to be actualised. Understanding the words does not add up to change, but *living* what you understand gives both substance and meaning to change.

And remember, no matter how you try . . . you cannot change and remain the same!

Michael J. Roads

Queensland, Oz

The thirty-one days of the month of

JANUARY

Thought for the month:

Most people believe in birth as the beginning and death as the ending of their life on earth.

This belief is part of life's illusion, cradling the fears that are so common in humanity.

Better to see life as endless continuity, rather like the frames in a reel of film. Each frame is a physical lifetime . . . and the movie of Self continues into eternity.

January 1st

One year ending, and another beginning is simply a cyclical calendar event. Life is, and should be lived, as an endless spiral in the continuity of Self.

People are seduced by the passing years. We believe in them. We move from one year into the next so totally unaware of our greater spiritual potential, of greater realities, of Self, that the years of our life just cycle along.

Cycles! Without our ever realising it, we are drifting along in one cycle after another. Any reading of world history will convince you that war, famine, repression and tyranny all happen in fairly regular cycles of human history. A cycle means more-of-the-same, endlessly repeating itself, our human cycles separated only by the illusion of time.

Make a New Year resolution to get off that cycle of sameness. You were born to live on the endless spiral of life. And a spiral never repeats itself. Resolve to spiral into newness this New Year. You can best accomplish this by the simple everyday process of constantly and consciously . . . choosing Love!

*Wisdom is the distillation of experience
and intelligence.*

Everyone has experience: everyone has
intelligence, yet not everyone has wisdom.
I could be kind and say that, yes, everyone has
wisdom, but comparatively few people use it;
it changes little!

Wisdom comes from an awareness of the little
things of life. Wisdom knows that the big things
of life are but a congregation of the little things.
Collectively, this is experience.

To find your own wisdom, focus on life in the
moment and live it without judgement. Realise
that life is an eternity event, and that you need
to acquire an eternity view. A single life-frame in
your life-movie gives a very limited view of reality
compared to holistically seeing the whole movie,
'The Continuity of Self'.

January 3rd

Wisdom is the difference between a 'separate' and a 'holistic' relationship with life.

While you look at life on a 'one life only' basis, it is difficult to obtain true wisdom.

There are several levels to wisdom. As a boy I thought that my father was wise, but now, as I see life from a holistic viewpoint, I see that his wisdom was based in making the best of the world of illusion. He too was a man of aphorisms, and just as some of them were truly ageless wisdom, so many were short-term in their application to life.

For example, his money aphorisms were based on financial security – short term, but his farmer wisdom based in the land was enduring. So often he told me, "A farmer's footsteps are the best fertiliser the land will ever receive." When I was a farmer, I certainly learned the wisdom of this. And obviously I inherited his love of aphorisms!

Wisdom is to intelligence and soul, as knowledge is to the intellect and mind.

Most people aspire to knowledge, whether it be general or specialised. Our knowledge is then integrated into our lives, literally becoming a part of our character and personality. Learning is mostly about intellectual stimulation, along with developing and improving the mind.

During a single lifetime a person can acquire a lot of knowledge. When, and if, this knowledge is used in such a way that not only that person, but many other people benefit, then the knowledge has been used wisely.

This, then, is the acquisition of wisdom. Over many such lifetimes in our life-movie, this wisdom connects deeply with the soul, and we develop an inherent wisdom that is with us on a spiritual level always.

It is wise to consciously . . . choose Love!

January 5th

There is no such thing as extinction.

This is not easy to explain! All life is One continuous flow of conscious intelligence in expression. Whereas linear time dominates our personal lives, in a greater metaphysical reality, linear time is of little consequence.

When a person dies, they pass out of our time frame. We say they are dead. And gone! When a whole species passes out of our time frame, we call that extinction. Gone! Just as a person continues in their life-movie 'The Continuity of Self', so also the species continue in the great life-movie 'The Continuity of Nature'.

Life can take a species expression beyond our immediate physical awareness, but it never takes a species expression beyond a metaphysical reality. Extinction is illusion. Life IS.

Expensive is not always better; inexpensive does not always mean cheap.

Some people are very impressed by the more expensive things of life, convinced that in this way they are being more successful.

An inexpensive car will take you on the same journey as an expensive car, and with less self-pretension. Inexpensive does not always mean lesser.

Walking in my garden on a hot day, I put on an expensive silk shirt for sun protection. In minutes I was soaked in sweat, the shirt stuck to me. I changed it for a inexpensive cotton shirt, remaining cooler, and far more comfortable.

Be sensible in life, using *appropriate* as the measure of what you use and invest in.

It is always appropriate to . . . choose Love!

January 7th

What you believe and expect becomes the substance of your life.

Have you examined your belief system lately? Do you have any unrealistic expectations? Both your beliefs and expectations become the window through which you view your life. Beliefs in particular become the aperture through which life flows. The very last thing that most people need is the manifestation of their erroneous beliefs and expectations.

What you focus on you attract. You may believe that life is difficult – I hope not – but I doubt you want to attract that as a reality. Equally, you may have some undesirable expectations, so be very careful. Sort through your beliefs and expectations and release any that do not honour you fully.

It honours you to consciously . . . choose Love!

Life supports true reality, not illusions. Illusions are, in fact, lifeless.

Most people live their lives overshadowed by the illusions of a personal reality. They have far less interaction with a greater reality. People believe that what we do in this moment will affect only our future; this is an illusion. What we do in this moment has as great an impact on our past as it does on our future, directly influencing our present moment. The reason that so many people struggle against life is that they live within ongoing illusions.

Life cannot support illusions, for they are without life. The energy for their continuity comes directly from you, not from the illusion of external life.

Expand the mind. Expand your view of life, and release strongly held opinions. Be ever open and flexible. Flexibility always . . . chooses Love!

January 9th

In the centre of all illusion, is Truth.

S eems like a paradox? It is. Nothing can deny Truth. Every time the falsities and illusions of life seem to overwhelm you, there is always an opportunity to see right into the heart of the situation and realise that Truth has not deserted you.

When you are confused and disorganised, illusion will prevail: when you are clear and ordered, Truth will stand revealed. Turmoil or order? This is a choice we make continually by the way we live.

Truth is consciously . . . choosing Love!

Attachment is the lock on the prison of desire.

Yes. Desire is a prison! An old saying goes like this: That which you most desire shall enslave you in the end. Very true.

Oddly, the things that we desire hold very little appeal once we have them, but desire continually whets its appetite for more. We get very attached to both the idea and the subsequent manifestation of our deep desires, yet our attachment to desire invariably has a price of disappointment and dissatisfaction.

Avoid the cycle of perpetual wants, the desire for this or that. If you really need it, get it. There is a big difference between real needs and baseless desires.

We truly need to . . . choose Love!

JANUARY 11th

Life flows at its best along the lines of timing,
probabilities, and appropriateness.

Life flows along the lines of probability. Our whole life is made up of probabilities, yet this is mostly unrecognised. The repeat factor is our dominant probability, especially if we harbour unresolved issues.

If our probability pattern is negative, it would be far better for us to move our life onto a path that is more appropriate for our inner growth and overall well-being.

With adequate intent, attention and effort, we can refocus ourselves, leaving behind the deep rut of negative probabilities, moving smoothly onto the path of positive potential.

This may require some practice, but it all goes more smoothly if we consciously . . . choose Love!

*The situation you are in – now – is the very substance
of your growth.*

You ou may not like the situation you are in, but
you created it, and you can benefit from it.
First, pay attention to all the positives in your
situation, and then work with them, building anew.

Odd as it may seem, most people focus on the
negatives, then oppose them, creating more stress
and suffering.

Truly, nothing in life ever works against you. But
you, of course, can work against life. This means
working against yourself.

Turn this around. Accept the growth that is on
offer, work *with* your situation, not *against,* and be
aware of, and grateful for the blessings it always
confers.

It is *with* life to always . . . choose Love!

JANUARY 13th

When you trust, Self negative probabilities decrease, while positive probabilities both increase and are empowered.

The choice is always yours, but you are required to trust Self before you can make a real choice to trust! A paradox?

Trusting Self is powerful. Trust creates a whole new scenario of possibilities. Many of the automatic negative repetitions of life simply cease, while new positive ideas and insights unfold into your awareness.

To trust Self is not a concept to think about; it is a reality to act upon.

It helps never to look on self as the 'little' self. This reduces your self esteem. Instead, focus on your greatness.

Your greatness always . . . chooses Love!

Conclusions are closed doors, while acceptable speculation holds them open.

Once you reach a conclusion, you move into the stagnant zone of thinking. You close the door on further speculation.

Knowing that you *know* is very different – and rare! The people who *think* they know makes statements like, "Well, this is the way it is." They believe in their conclusions, and are inclined to cling to them. Their belief becomes very personal and they vigorously defend it.

Be open. You do not need to come to a final conclusion. You can reach an acceptable speculation, open to its being proven correct or incorrect without any attachment to it, and without taking any of it personally.

And if you should be wrong it presents a perfect opportunity to consciously . . . choose Love!

January 15th

Mind will support your confusion, but life always supports your trust.

You will find that I often mention trust.

It is probably the most self-empowering action you can express. When you trust life you trust self; when you trust self you are on the road to creating an uplifting and self-supporting life.

Remember, mind revels in your mental detritus, unconcerned by the intellectual confusion that has been generated.

Let go of all the mental 'working it out', and simply trust in your own heartfelt or intuitive decision making.

Intuition consciously . . . chooses Love!

Illusion is a game in the mind.

Powerful and hypnotic, the mind spins games and illusions, and people call the resulting mixture – life.

One way out is simply to relax about things. Most of what you get stressed over does not even matter in the greater, overall expression of your life.

You cannot rid yourself forcibly of the illusion game, nor can you turn it off. But you can cease to take it, or yourself quite so seriously.

Relax in the knowledge that one day you will pierce the illusion – this is your birthright – meanwhile growing gently, and strongly – not forcibly – toward that moment of inner illumination.

It is illuminating to always . . . choose Love!

January 17th

Supporting the illusions of life is a poor deal, because the illusions will not support you.

I have found often that if I offer an observation to someone about one of the illusions in their life, they argue in favour of keeping it. Not a good idea!

The illusions of life are very subtle, disguised and hidden in the clothing of apparent truth and reality. But they are not supportive of you as a spiritual Being.

Generally, you learn of the illusions in your life only when you have the potential to release them. This requires you to be flexible, open, and non-attached.

Choosing Love is super-supportive.

Every judgement and criticism you make of yourself will prove to be unworthy of you.

You are worth far more than you realise.

Self-judgement or criticism will never reveal your true worth, all they will do is seriously devalue you. And you deserve better than that. A state of innocence never makes a judgement.

If you view yourself with appreciation and respect, then you will find the real value and true worth of yourself.

This also works in relation to family, other people, and life in general.

High self-esteem always . . . chooses Love!

January 19th

Your beliefs shape the way you think, yet your thoughts shape your beliefs!

t makes you wonder which came first!

Obviously thoughts have to precede our beliefs, to give them shape and meaning, yet it is those beliefs that then shape the way we think.

This is not necessarily a good cycle to get locked into. Once we have constructed a strong belief, we have created a life-box that will contain and limit our thinking. Let go of the need for beliefs, or, if this is not possible for you, release your attachment to the beliefs.

Non-attachment is one of the major requirements to be practised along the path of spiritual enlightenment. Along with the art of consciously . . . choosing Love!

Without focus or direction, thought is a vast oceanic current going nowhere.

Few people realise the true power of thought. Books are written on the subject, and read, but the true reality seldom sinks in – our thoughts give meaning and shape to our lives.

The vast majority of people think their thoughts without any awareness of what those thoughts are creating, or where their thoughts might lead them.

Your thoughts are a vast power. You either direct that power, or you let it run wild.

Put simply, wild means confusion in your life, while directed thought can be used for your greater benefit.

Your choice is in your thinking. Think about it, and . . . choose Love.

January 21st

Let go of the idea that what we see in other people –
positive or negative – does not apply to ourselves.

Our view of other people often reflects an unrecognised, sometimes unwanted inner view. When we see the positive qualities of another person, we are also seeing our own inner positivity.

Unfortunately, most people are more attuned to the negative, easily seeing this expression in other people.

If you look for the positive qualities in life, they will be expressed in you. In a like manner, if you look for the negative issues in life, these too will become your expression.

The good news is . . . you can choose!
Try . . . choosing Love!

The main expression of sameness is to create fear,
because fear will always defend and maintain
more-of-the-same.

More-of-the-same is not the essence of life.
Rather, more-of-the-same is a denial of life,
it's stagnation, yet this subconscious conformity
with our past is the comfort of the masses. Life is
about newness, not the repetition of the past, yet
most people avoid the new, preferring more-of-the-
same.

Even when this conformity is painful, it holds the
comfort of habit, and people hang on.

To the degree that you can attain, let go of the
endless repetitions in your life. Open the door
to newness, knowing that if you can do this and
embrace the new fully, it will be for your ultimate
benefit as a spiritual Being.

It is new to consciously . . . choose Love!

January 23rd

If you walk the path of risk practising unconditional trust, then you are no longer walking the path of risk!

What is a risk? If you live in the world of illusion a risk is easy to define: anything that threatens life, limb, or livelihood. If, however, you know the Truth of Self, then you realise that risk is no more than an old attachment to the illusion of so-called safety and security.

Never let a risk dictate or determine the way you live. Within the bounds of sensibility trust unconditionally . . . and keep on trusting, no matter what transpires.

Eventually, risk will be exposed as the impostor it is.

There is no risk if you . . . choose Love!

Memory is based in understanding.
Understanding, however, is more based
in conception and perception than it is in reality.

What we *think* we know is far different than the reality of knowing! We may have a concept of a certain fact, but the reality of that fact still eludes us.

People often say to me, "I understand," but if I then ask them to explain it to me, they are very uncertain.

Be aware that while understanding life on a physical and intellectual level is a requirement for everyday life, trying to understand your spiritual life is a waste of time and effort. Trust your wisdom-Self . . . until you *know* that you *know!*

Knowing consciously . . . chooses Love!

January 25th

When you treat yourself as though you are a King, or Queen, then life will fill in all the entitlements.

Most people think of themselves personally in terms of *less* rather than in terms of *more*. Trust me, you are far, far more than you realise – far more than you credit yourself with being.

Think of yourself and treat yourself in terms of being a King, or Queen. It may stretch your self-esteem to do this, but if you do, and you persevere, you should not be too surprised when life treats you accordingly.

In the way that you constantly think of yourself, life will meet you on those terms. Think beautiful, and magnificent! Think in terms of always . . . choosing Love!

When you are open to life, then life will present new openings.

How can you expect new opportunities if you are closed to life? Take each day as a brand new opportunity to be ever more open to life, ever more receptive.

Life responds to openness and receptivity. Being open to life means being open without any agenda of expectation.

Open means simply that – open to life. No expectation, no desires, just an openness to what the day might offer.

Nature lives this way, but it is rare in humans. Openness . . . chooses Love!

January 27th

The only heart that is naturally open to giving is the heart that has been opened by receiving.

Many people give. Some give that they may receive recognition, while others give to help their self-esteem.

Some give from pity, or sympathy, and some that they might be seen to give. Some, of course, give because they have an open, loving, caring heart.

And then there is receiving! There are those who have had to learn to receive that they might continue to live.

It is only by someone receiving that another person can give. Sometimes the greatest gift that you can give a person is to gratefully and gracefully receive.

You gift to yourself by . . . choosing Love!

Spiritual enlightenment is not an acquisition;
it is a surrender.

Some people pursue enlightenment. This is foolish, because enlightenment is not running away. Spiritual enlightenment is not to be found outside Self, so the pursuit is about chasing a concept, an illusion. Stop attempting to gain something, and surrender to the ever-new Now.

Everything that you seek, everything for which your heart and soul most longs, is to be found in the eternal moment.

It is to the fullness and immense richness of this moment that you surrender.

Do it . . . now! Just let go.

It is enlightening to . . . choose Love!

January 29th

The days of your life are the playing-fields of self-expression.

It is often said that life is the stage and that we are the actors.

Look at it in another way. Your whole physical life is based in the playing-fields of linear time. In linear time you can play any game you like, from money making to pain making, but the greatest game is discovering and expressing your beautiful true Self.

However, you are free to play at any game you wish, for no matter how seriously you take it, a game is a game!

I suggest that the common game of suffering has never been necessary; most certainly it is no longer appropriate.

Try playing at . . . choosing Love!

Criticism and adverse judgement take families apart, while acceptance and deep appreciation bring families together.

How odd people are.
We all know that this aphorism is true, yet why do so few people live the latter way?

Begin with your own family. Ignore all that you could so easily criticise, and focus on all that you can possibly appreciate.

You will soon find that acceptance and appreciation reap a harvest of Love, while criticism and adverse judgement create and spread the blight of sorrow.

Adverse judgement is poor judgement!

Appreciation always . . . chooses Love!

The less the thinking, the greater the clarity.

Psychologists say that most people think at the rate of two to three hundred words a minute . . . and mostly nonsense!

I have met people who are shocked to learn that they can hold their breath for longer than they can stop their thinking.

Thoughts should not be denied, but neither do they need to be cultivated all day long.

The more you focus into the *doing* and *being* of your moment-by-moment life, the slower and less demanding are your thoughts. If you must think, then think about consciously . . . choosing Love!

The twenty-eight days of the month of

FEBRUARY

[with the 29th day of a Leap Year]

Thought for the month:

Most people see their daily life in terms of good or bad, right or wrong, and all the grey shades in between.

Better to look at your life as an ongoing interpretation of the 'script of life' that you are writing for yourself.

It is within your every moment of life that you write this script.

FEBRUARY 1st

Every repetitive self-criticism is a step away from the magnificent toward the mediocre.

Why is the magnificent in you so much more difficult to embrace and accept than the mediocre? How often do you tell anyone that you – and they – are magnificent?

Why not? Why do we become focussed on criticism so very easily, while appreciation seems such a struggle? It began with all of us, each generation, as a child, but it is as a conscious adult that we must end it.

You are magnificent; this is Truth. Any criticism – especially if continuous – of self or others, is a tarnish on yourself and life. Instead of tarnishing your life . . . polish it.

Choosing Love is an excellent polish!

Overindulgence of your children is the slow erosion of their self-worth.

If, as a child, everything comes to us without any effort on our part, we learn to be helpless and dependent.

When, as an adult, that helplessness is exposed by our inability to function capably and efficiently under the stress and pressure of everyday life, our self-worth plummets.

If you are a victim of this situation, then you need to volunteer deliberately for jobs or situations that will challenge and stretch you. Have confidence that you can meet and conquer such challenges.

It is a challenge to always . . . choose Love!

FEBRUARY 3rd

Juvenile responsibility is the initiation of self-worth.

It is so easy to give gifts unceasingly to our children in a mistaken belief that this is an act of Love. It is not.

The great gift that we can give them is a gift that takes many years to develop. It is that most priceless of gifts, one that will last their lifetime and smooth their passage along their path in life. This is the gift of high self-worth.

This means that throughout all their years of 'growing up' the child is given increasing and appropriate responsibility according to the needs of the family and the ability of the child. In this way you guide them toward a life of consciously . . . choosing Love!

Self-worth begins in childhood, not as an adult.

I meet so many people with low self-worth, low self-esteem. In just about every person it was either denied or destroyed as a child by overdoses of criticism.

In these people a damaged child is hiding, lost somewhere in the persons psyche. Find this inner child, and together, child and adult, learn how to reestablish the child's worth. If you rebuild the self-esteem of the inner child, you rebuild your adult life.

This is not as difficult as it may seem. Through meditation, or inner exploration, this child is waiting to be rediscovered and resurrected into your daily life.

If you can achieve this, the extra power that is released into your life, as the inner child is healed, has to be experienced to be believed.

To finalise the healing . . . choose Love!

February 5th

Continuous self-criticism and hardship mostly live together.

Hardship has its expression in many forms. You may continuously criticise yourself and be wealthy, but you will encounter hardship in some other form – probably in relationships.

The chronic and repetitive nature of adverse criticism induces hardship by creating an ongoing negative focus and bias.

The focus of criticism is based in *what is wrong*, meaning that wrongness, or adversity, is attracted to such a person.

Give up adverse criticism and focus on the many blessings in your life. In this way you create more!

A constant blessing is . . . choosing Love!

Enthusiasm is the birthplace of accomplishment.

To be enthusiastic means to be God-filled. Little wonder that if you are enthusiastic about life and living, you will accomplish much.

Enthusiasm is usually an innate gift, but it is certainly possible to develop it.

To achieve this you need to find a career or hobby in your life that gives you great enjoyment. This can be the precursor to true enthusiasm.

Another way of igniting enthusiasm is by developing a genuine enjoyment of Nature, people, and life.

Enthusiasm grows by . . . choosing Love!

FEBRUARY 7th

All too often aggressive thoughts attract violent situations.

Monitor your thoughts occasionally and you might be surprised at how aggressive they can be. So many people in situations of violence are those who think often with anger. Getting angry about world violence is literally connecting the thinker to the violence. And it finds us.

While it is possible in our world of thought to release some inner tension by 'thinking it through', we must be careful to avoid anger creeping into these thoughts. Such thoughts generate more tension, along with an unhealthy focus that is attracting either physical, emotional, or mental violence into our life.

Loving and forgiving thoughts are a powerful and safe avenue to inner release. It is very powerful to consciously . . . choose Love!

Thought and reality are one and the same.

The reality you are in is the reality you have created. If you like it, congratulations, if you do not, then I suggest you change it.

How? By changing the content and focus of your thoughts.

Illusion is looking at life as good or bad, right or wrong. Nothing is good or bad, right or wrong; the way you think makes it so!

Remember that you live what you create. Your thoughts need to be your creative power in conscious action.

Pay attention to what it is that you *do* want in life, not to what you do *not* want. Focus on what is enjoyable in your life, not on what makes you miserable. Continually entertain the thoughts that allow you to feel uplifted and happy.

Think Love, and consciously . . . choose Love!

February 9th

You cannot make new changes if you are enslaved by old programs.

People generally like the idea of changes being a feature in their life, but only a few actually implement them. Mostly, we avoid real change. Some people even move house, but in their daily living it is only the surroundings that get changed, while their life continues its usual routine.

When the conditioning of a lifetime is really strong, we follow an inherent program that we don't even realise exists.

This is not easy to escape, but it is not impossible.

First, you must recognise the deep conditioning program, then introduce experiences into your life that directly confront it. This will shatter your comfort zone, allowing you the more easily to move toward new changes.

You change by always . . . choosing Love!

Joy and fulfilment in the moment is the
place of magic.

Most people no longer believe in magic. I do. A lack of belief is usually an adult affliction.

Magic occupies only a single place in life, but that place occupies all that is . . . the dynamic moment. When you find joy and happiness in the moment – and this is your creation – you are experiencing magic.

Although children have the ability to do this naturally and easily, fewer are doing so. As we move into an age that offers the distraction of ever more electronic gadgets, we move our children ever further from the serendipitous encounters with the natural magic of Nature.

Life is pure magic when you . . . choose Love!

FEBRUARY 11th

Whatever it is in life that seems to be working against you, in the exact same proportion it is also working for you.

We are quick to condemn, quick to criticise, quick to see what we consider is wrong with life. Our focus has become short-term, seldom open to the benefits that may be accruing.

As I look back on the times of pain and suffering in my life, I am aware it was exactly that which led to my spiritual enlightenment.

Everything in my daily life that I used to resist was always working for me, offering me an opportunity to be more open, more flexible, and to develop the wisdom of insight.

The little, short-term view of life is too clouded with self-pity to embrace a greater reality. It seldom occurs to us that what is apparently going wrong, may, in the longer term, be unfolding gloriously right.

You will 'know' life's Truth only when you no longer need to know it.

The people who actively search for life's Truth are few, because you have to live the reality of your search. You cannot search for Truth with the mind, for Truth is neither conceptual nor intellectual.

To find Truth you surrender the search. Instead, you develop an awareness and appreciation of Truth being expressed in your every moment of life. By doing this, you discover that you and life's Truth are One, and that it has always been this way. This is simple enough to do, but not easy!

Life and Truth consciously . . . express Love!

FEBRUARY 13th

Truth cannot be explained, nor can it be given to you. You cannot take Truth, or hold it, or in any way control it.

This Truth of which I write of is the basic Principle of Life. It is the very foundation upon which life is based. And life is, first and foremost, an *eternal* expression of spirit.

To embrace Truth within yourself is to surrender to Self. The desire for Truth will forever deny it, for desire can never meet Truth.

Life's Truth is a state of consciousness, a place so over full and yet so utterly empty, that it defies all rationality. Nor is Truth logical.

But then . . . neither is Self!

However, it is wise *and* logical to . . . choose Love!

Love is not an emotion. Love is the power of creation being expressed through humanity.

There is our normal daily love, and there is unconditional Love. We emotionalise and dramatise love. Our concepts of love are mostly acquired young, from observing our parents, watching movies, television, and reading. Quite a mixed bag!

Unconditional Love is rare. Very rare. Mostly we achieve the 'I love you, if you love me' type of love, and that's fine. But we do need to move on from there.

The Love that is most important in your life is unconditional Love for yourself. This is the deepest, truest way that you can experience Love. And it is the most difficult.

But not if, in your everyday life, you constantly and consciously . . . choose Love!

FEBRUARY 15th

Habits create, maintain, defend, and rationalise habits.

In one way or another, we are all creatures of habit. A habit of regular meditation is supportive, while a drug or alcohol habit is destructive.

Unfortunately we have too few supportive habits, compared with the many ruinous ones.

You cannot remove a bad habit and simply leave a vacuum. The only way to remove a bad habit is consciously to replace it with a good one.

'Being conscious' is the key factor. Habits are subconscious, happening without our conscious awareness. It is only by being consciously aware in the moment-by-moment of life that we can remove a habit does not honour us.

It is odd, but true, that if you *consciously* choose Love on a daily basis it is not habit, but a wise and *conscious* choice.

If you support a bad habit, be aware that the
habit will not support you.

It really is amazing what people will do to support
a bad habit. A drug or alcohol habit illustrates this
very well.

Withdraw your support from a habit that offers
you nothing but suffering or grief.

First, identify the habit you no longer want, then
decide on action. And you must follow through
whatever you decide to do. Despite all the medical
aids for breaking addictions, nothing will be fully
effective until you have reached a firm decision
that you are going to end the habit.

Replace all habits by . . . choosing Love!

FEBRUARY 17th

The mind cannot set you free, for it does not imprison you. Your long-conditioned thoughts and beliefs are what the mind serves.

So many people believe that the mind and intellect are the paths to spiritual freedom.

They are wrong. Despite the way it seems, it is an illusion that mind has ever imprisoned you. The conditioning of your thoughts have created beliefs that support illusion: one such illusion is that we are imprisoned.

This is a very powerful illusion.

Mind will serve this belief, despite the fact that such a belief may hold our so-called death.

Mind has no experience of death, so does not fear it. Fear resides with ego/identity.

Clearly know that Self has never been imprisoned. This means that you are free the moment you consciously claim your freedom.

Mind always serves, never commands, yet
because of our ego-centred reality, it appears
that mind is our master. This is an illusion.

People know so little about mind. It may
sound arrogant to say that the commonly
accepted description of the mind is not correct,
but nevertheless, it is in error. The relationship
between the mind and human survives after death,
with the self-created illusions continuing.

Those on their spiritual path often get the idea
that they have to defeat the mind, but this is not
so. When your relationship with yourself is truly
based in Love, and Self is Realised, mind is no
longer in opposition.

And you know that it never was!

FEBRUARY 19th

Mind cannot program itself. Our thoughts and emotions create the program.

Be careful what you think! These words have been written and spoken many times, and they remain very true. It is a pity so few people take any notice of them!

Whatever is going on in the mind, beneficial or harmful, your own thinking has created and set the program. Moreover – this is not a pleasant thought – you came into this life with the continuing program from your previous incarnation. Turn your thoughts toward a real acceptance of yourself, other people and life. In this way you begin the reprogramming of your eternity.

A good start is to . . . choose Love!

Truth always remains constant as Truth, but only within a person's own perfect timing can Truth be recognised, accepted, and acted upon.

You may read a Truth in this book that is out of timing for you. In that case you are likely to reject it, thinking that I am wrong. This is, of course, your prerogative, but it changes nothing in regard to Truth. Truth remains Truth, while your ability to grow with it is put on hold.

To be open to Truth is to be open to inner growth. Does the tulip bulb know of the beautiful flower that awaits to be expressed, or is its reality simply one of continuing growth.

It is a wise truth to consciously . . . choose Love!

A key to spiritual growth is in being 'aware'.

The more you experience of life on a metaphysical level, the greater will be your *aware* experience. The greater your aware experience, the more you will experience of life on a metaphysical level.

Equally, the greater your metaphysical experience of life becomes, so, in proportion your physical experience will become deeper, creating a more meaningful interface with life.

The greater your interface with life, so also you will have a far deeper relationship with yourself. And it strengthens your will to . . . choose Love!

Repetitive thoughts create the overall theme of your life.

When you lower your vibrational frequency through continuous negative thinking, you give expression to misfortune, confusion, and discord in your life at an ever increasing and accelerating intensity.

Similarly, when you raise your vibrational frequency through higher, Loving and self-appreciative thoughts, so you create an ever increasing measure of good fortune, clarity, and harmony for yourself.

Be aware of what your repetitive thought-focus is targeting. Target . . . choosing Love!

FEBRUARY 23rd

Pain is a learned reaction.

When we injure ourselves, or get hurt, the first thing we do is focus on the expected pain . . . and we get it. Our imagination helps to create pain because we have learned to expect it.

When, at a seminar, I had two of my fingers shut in the hinge side of a heavy door, they were badly crushed – the pain excruciating. I laid down on a settee, closed my eyes and immediately went into an altered state of consciousness. I directed my imagination away from the pain, visualising the pain flowing out of my fingertips in a wave of pink light energy.

Within ten minutes there was absolutely no pain – fingers still crushed – and I was able to continue the seminar.

Despite this . . . I still have an injection at the dentists to numb the pain!

If you are willing to take a risk in your life,
there are no risks. If, however, you are
afraid to take risks, then life is very risky!

More paradox. Truth is like that! This is, once
again, a matter of attraction. If you take a risk
easily, then risks hold little or no fear for you, thus
risks are minimised.

If, however, you are afraid to take a risk, living your
life as safely and securely as possible, then the
fear of risks will have the effect of magnifying and
magnetising risks.

Take the risks that need to be taken with as little
concern as possible. Trust in your ability to deal
capably with life. And continue to consciously . . .
choose Love!

Self-mastery comes on all levels, and seldom the more obvious.

Some people – a minority – look for spiritual growth. This is to be encouraged and respected.

However, if this is your quest, do not ignore your emotional and physical life, nor the focus and quality of your thinking.

Many people believe that spiritual growth is something that you pursue, or learn. It is not. It is a state of consciousness that is the result of living your life as a *conscious* spiritual Being.

Let go of trying to be a better person, because this also holds the belief that you are not good enough, right now.

In Truth, you are . . . when you *know* you are!

Joy comes from within. It is the result of a
Loving in-the-moment relationship between
identity-self and soul-self.

Most people today seek joy on an external
level. People no longer know the difference
between joy, happiness and pleasure.

Pleasure seeking does not create true joy or real
happiness. We can laugh, be caught up in the
illusions that pleasures offer, but it all proves to be
so fleeting. A fun movie does not make us joyful or
happy, anymore than the laughter from too much
alcohol.

We find *real* joy and happiness when, inside
ourselves, there is so much appreciation and
fulfilment and Love in being the person whom we
are, that joy and happiness shines within.

We create inner joy by . . . choosing Love!

February 27th

Each person holds an infinite number of probabilities in the continuing moment of life's infinite expression through you.

Life is not about destiny and fate. If it were there would be no free will. Life is about the endless probabilities that can be expressed in each moment of your life.

Once you get into a rut or your life is ruled by habits, then the probability is that this will continue. Obviously, attachments create the probabilities of sameness.

To express the probability with your greatest potential requires you to be open, flexible, optimistic, and without attachments.

Nothing creates a greater probability future than one of consciously . . . choosing Love!

You will not thrive and prosper even in the midst of plenty, if that plenty does not contain the needs of the soul-self you truly are.

There are but few who look to the needs of the soul-self they are, as paramount in their lives. To do this does not require a pious attitude but rather, a joyful and optimistic one.

To thrive and prosper is to be united with life in an overall inner harmony.

If there is inner harmony, invariably it is expressed in a physical reality of abundance.

Consider your deeper needs, rather than simply the fleeting 'wants' that so easily dominate and distract you in your daily life.

Let the needs of the soul-self you are have a more powerful place in your life.

You grow in power by . . . choosing Love!

February 29th ... a Leap year.

We never really expect the unexpected.
Not even when it is a regular event with
irregular timing.

G rowing up in England, I learned that about one
summer in ten, give or take a few years, was
blazing hot and dry. So it was with winter, when
once every decade or so, it was exceptionally cold.
And each time, summer or winter, people died
from the climatic extremes. It still happens!

We never seem to learn that just because an event
is only occasional, it does not mean that it will not
happen again. It is unwise to dismiss and forget
such irregular events.

Without any fear or alarm, or any negativity, it is
wise to be prepared for the unexpected.

The thirty-one days of the month of

MARCH

Thought for the month:

Most people blame themselves, or other people when things appear to go wrong, or they get hurt.

Better not to view life in terms of blame, but rather to accept responsibility for yourself, and the situation that you are in.

March 1st

All of a persons life is a probability, and the
probability is that very few will ever realise this.

Most people think that in their life anything can happen. This is seldom true. Lifetime following lifetime we are creating a template of probabilities, and in each life that template holds an ever more probable definition of the way that we, individually, will live.

This is the prison in which humanity is caged, and the probability is that it will continue. You do, of course, have the option to break the probability template, if first you have accepted its reality.

You break the template by treating yourself with the honour and respect that you would accord to a Goddess, or a God.

It also helps to consciously . . . choose Love!

Correct focus allows desired potentials to become possible realities.

If you are reading my insights daily, you will by now be aware of what subconscious focus creates. It creates everything in your life that you do not want.

Your conscious attention on the strengths and qualities that are inherent in you will allow your greatest potential to become a reality.

Most thoughts flicker and flare like a candle in the wind. Conscious and focused thinking needs be a constant flame, fed by your optimism and maintained by your awareness.

March 3rd

Inflexibility is the death of expansion.

Life for all of us is about expansion and growth. This is a process of continuity, not something that only happens when we are young. Young bodies grow up, reach maturity, then, with age, become ever more rigid and inflexible. It does not have to be this way.

Consider the person who grows up keeping the mind and thoughts open and optimistic, who is not afraid of constant change, and who welcomes each new day for its new potential, and its new opportunities for the miraculous.

Such a person remains flexible in attitude and body. Such a person will find it easy to constantly and consciously . . . choose Love!

Joy is the tangible expression of Love.

I can remember when, on my spiritual path, the very moment I learned that I had never experienced what joy truly is. That moment had a great impact on me. I had been very happy, but being happy is not the full expression of deep inner joy.

Joy is impossible to truly define. Among the meanings in a mid-twentieth century dictionary, we find, 'a beloved one', 'to exult', 'rapture'.

I agree. When we exult in our Love for our Beloved Creator, then our joy becomes such that it paints its very essence into the every-moment canvas of our lives.

This . . . is joy . . . is Love!

March 5th

For most people, Truth is a tiny egg in a very large material nest.

Every person has the seed of Truth within them. Some people are aware of this, many are not. The preoccupation of most people is to line their nest with a great amount of material wealth. Within this type of nest, Truth is usually of little real concern.

It is natural enough to build your nest, but it is prudent and wise to also nurture the tiny egg of Truth.

The time will come when the nest has lost its value, and all that will be of significance is the egg. Materialism or Truth: these do not need to be naturally exclusive, but you do need to keep a clear perspective on the long term values.

Love . . . is a good nest lining!

Truth cannot be reduced to words. Truth, when spoken, is not the experience of Truth. At best, words are signposts pointing to where Truth may be found and experienced.

Truth is life in manifestation and expression.

A rabbit has no problems with its Truth. It has no illusions about what it is to be a rabbit. In its own way, it knows and expresses Truth.

Humans however, do have a problem with Truth, and they live within a constant illusion about what it is to be a human.

People are so busy being *human that* they have no time to ponder the Truth of a human *being!*

When you find the signposts that hold meaning for you, and they point you toward Truth, you would be wise to take that direction.

A wise direction is . . . choosing Love!

MARCH 7th

Truth is always found within Self, yet it is only truly found when the searcher ceases the search.

Knowing Self is to know Truth. Remember, when I write self, I refer to the identity-self.

When I write Self in this way, I refer to the enlightened-Self. It is within Self that Truth is to be found. And here we have the paradox: if you maintain the desire to know Self, you will not find Self, yet equally, without the desire to know Self, you will not find Self.

There is a way past this catch-22 situation. Once you *know* that your life will never be complete without knowing Self, let go of the desire. Simply live your life in a way that honours Self. This withdraws energy from the stranglehold of desire, while taking you toward Self.

*Balance is the meeting place between discord
and harmony.*

D o not be fooled into thinking that balance
is about being undisturbed and blissful.
To be balanced is to allow the discord of life its
expression without being stressed, and to be
unattached to harmony.

Let harmony be an important part of your life, but
not at the cost of denying discord. Denying discord
is counterproductive.

Accept discord as part of the orchestration of
life. By flowing with it, rather than moving into
opposition, you will find the deeper base rhythm
of inner harmony. This is the place of balance.
Balance is easily found when you constantly and
consciously . . . choose Love!

March 9th

Awareness reveals that which is hidden.

Most people only see and relate to the obvious in life. Walking with my son, Russell, is a good example of Nature awareness. He sees those creatures that for most people are hidden.

Within our lives there is so much hidden. Self is hidden behind the image and illusion of self, while the continuity of life is hidden behind the illusion of death.

So very much is hidden. The Nature we see and relate to is the physical manifestation of a deeper, hidden, metaphysical Nature. Although hidden from eyesight, it is not hidden from *in-sight*.

Develop a continuous and focussed awareness of life. Be open to the miraculous.

Miracles follow . . . consciously choosing Love!

The metaphysical precedes the physical.

This is one of the primary Truths of life.

Some people have problems even thinking about the metaphysical, but the simple reality is that life is first and foremost an expression of energy, and that energy is non-physical.

Metaphysical energy has a frequency that is faster than light, meaning that we are unable physically to see it.

Once the frequency becomes slower – physical – then it all becomes visible for us.

For most people, only when life is physically seen and apparent do they believe that it exists.

This limitation is one of the birthplaces of illusion. Grasp the fact that first and foremost you are a magnificent metaphysical Being of Love/Light.

March 11th

Life will always offer you the opportunity for more of who you have been, or, more of who you could be.

Let me be clear about this: more of *who you have been* is easy, while *more of who you could be* will challenge you. Moreover, life will offer far more of who you have been simply because life follows a probability pattern.

Your life is in your hands. If you want to develop a little – or maybe a lot – of who you could be, then, either as a self-employed or an employed person, or simply as a spiritual Being on your path, always look for work and/or life situations and opportunities that will challenge and stretch your current abilities, thus developing your greater potential.

It is a challenge to consciously . . . choose Love!

Self-appreciation reinforces the foundation of self.
Self-criticism reduces the foundation of self.

S elf-criticism is incredibly common. Much of the two to three hundred words a minute of everyday thinking is a subconscious criticism of yourself. Adverse comparing, judging, criticising, all this severely reduces the very foundation on which you build your life.

By contrast, self-appreciation both reinforces and strengthens the foundation of your life.

Why then, is this so rare?

As far as is practically possible, I recommend that you avoid all those people who regularly criticise other people, politicians, and world situations, and mix with the people who look for the best in other people and in life for what they can most appreciate. Look for those rare and beautiful people who . . . choose Love!

March 13th

Self-appreciation is constructive, while self-criticism is destructive. The choice-less choice of most people is self-criticism.

If you wish to become a new person, one whom you can honour and admire, you must consciously choose, and use, self-appreciation.

Conscious choice is the key. Being aware of your thinking and making a conscious choice to think thoughts that honour you, will rebuild and guide your life toward your inherent greatness.

You need to take back your power to choose.

Most people never make a choice of criticising or not criticising, they simply follow the program they received as a child from critical parents. This is choice-less choice. Choose appreciation! Choose Love!

To empower your Truth, you must live it.

Whether you use my insights on a daily basis or read them at random, everything you read and learn must be lived. If you simply read it and intellectually understand the words, the fact is you have gained and learned nothing.

Everything I have written in this book is my *knowing* of Truth. Nothing is written as a clever or intellectual statement. It is all comes from learned-by-living experiences within my life.

If you find Truth in your life, live it. Only in this way will Truth reveal its greater picture. It is a Truth to consciously . . . choose Love!

March 15th

Truth not lived is Truth not realised.

After an evening talk, people often say to me, "Now I have another part of the Truth." They look very pleased with this, referring to their fragment as one more piece in the overall perceived jigsaw puzzle of life.

Nothing could be further from the Truth! All they have is a mental concept of Truth. Truth has no fragments. It cannot be reduced to pieces, then put together like a puzzle. Truth is holistic. Its integrity is inviolate.

The only way that Truth can be an experience, or that Truth can be actually realised, is by living it. There is no other way.

You live it by always . . . choosing Love!

Poverty and starvation are extreme physical manifestations of self-denial. Abundance and well being are physical manifestations of self-acceptance.

We each create our own reality. Many people know the words, but few really comprehend what it truly means.

If you live within a continuous reality of self-denial, seeing self as something less than worthy, as insignificant, then this too must have its own eventual manifestation.

Of course, this is over many lifetimes of your life-movie.

If you accept that self/Self is a manifestation of God, that you are a divine expression of God – not separate – and you live in a manner that honours this reality, then abundance and wellbeing will characterise your life.

Yes . . . it is also about . . . choosing Love!

March 17th

There is no higher-Self and lower-self;
there is only Self.

As I have often written, Self is who you are. When I refer to self, this is the aspect that relates to separation and identity. Some people call this the ego-self. The problem with this is that these people often indulge in attacking their ego, claiming that the ego must die before Self can be realised.

This is nonsense.

It is Love that brings freedom from the illusion, and Love does not attack any aspect of who you are to achieve this.

Love and accept yourself for who you are, the way you are, right now. Treat identity-self lovingly, gently, and with great care.

Always, always, always . . . choose Love!

There is nothing outside Self.

This is a Truth that people at my evening talks and 5-Day Intensives have the most difficulty in consciously comprehending, or understanding. It is simple enough to write, but difficult to explain.

When you truly experience Self, when you are spiritually enlightened, you are aware that Self – energy – is All that Is.

Your relationship with space and time changes. This is not a physical change, but a change in your whole relationship with life.

Christ taught that the Kingdom of Heaven is within. This is the same sentiment in function, but very differently expressed.

Heaven is a state of consciousness; Self is a state of consciousness. The Kingdom of Heaven is within . . . Self.

To be fair, there are many other ways, or angles that I could use to explain this apparent paradox, and all are to do with energy.

MARCH 19th

Taking risks leads to the development of courage; courage is the path to self- confidence.

If you are aware that your whole life is an expression of the continuity of Self, and that despite the illusions of identity 'who you are' is not born, nor will 'who you are' die; if you are aware of this, then what is a risk?

Risks are a part of life. It is not wise to go looking for risks, but when life puts risks in your path they are there for a reason.

Some risks are there to test your courage, and must be faced, other risks are there to test your wisdom, and should be avoided.

Self-confidence is gained by making the right choices. Let your intuition make the choice!

Intuition consciously . . . chooses Love!

There are two simultaneous movies within your life;
Truth, the positive, and Illusion, the negative.

The movie that the vast majority of people see
and live is the movie of Illusion, but always the
movie of Truth is there, in each and every moment.
A focus on illusion will never reveal the movie of
Truth, but a focus on Truth will always penetrate
the movie of Illusion.

Of course, you have to be prepared to live this
focus, for the intellect will only intensify the
movie of Illusion. If, however, you live with an
aware focus, intelligence will always reinforce your
connection to Truth.

Intelligence always . . . chooses Love!

March 21st

Place your dreams in today, live them today, and you will see your dreams realised.

Dreams you have when asleep have their place in your life, but the dreams to which I refer are the dreams of achievement or ambition. Most of us have our dreams for the future, and that is exactly where they stay – in the future. A dream for the future cannot be a realised dream in the moment.

To the extent that you are able, live your dream now, in this moment. In every possible way bring it into your life. Think about how, in this moment, you can activate your dream, making it tangible and real, now. Imagine your dream becoming a reality.

If you place your dreams in the context of tomorrow you will never feel the creative joy of their expression, for tomorrow is part of the movie of illusion.

We all dream of things we want to happen, places we would enjoy to go. Dreams are part of what make us human.

However, in itself, dreams are not part of our everyday reality; they are something that we hope to eventually reach. This is where illusion comes in. *Eventually reach* is something that will never happen, for as we all know, tomorrow never comes.

Am now reaching is the path of reality, for this is the path of today. It is the same with: I am consciously . . . choosing Love!

MARCH 23rd

Honouring Self is both wise and powerful. It means that if you follow your spiritual path in an honouring way, your material needs will be met. If you follow only your material path, then your spiritual needs will be neglected.

When you honour Self, you honour your totality, the holistic you. This not only meets your natural spiritual needs, but it also includes your material needs. However, this path of honour is not the way that most people live.

Most people have a deep subconscious fear of not having enough, so they strive to get enough money, enough wealth, enough whatever to subvert that fear. This brings no satisfaction.

No matter how you deal with fear, everything that feeds it energy will empower it.

It is Self-honouring to . . . choose Love!

Bitterness is an acid that destroys first its own container.

A surprising number of people surreptitiously view others with bitterness. Without a doubt they think that they have a good reason, but they seldom realise that their bitterness is an attack on their own health.

I have talked to many people after public talks and during my 5-Day Intensives and have learned to recognise the various symptoms of bitterness.

Generally, such people have a litany of aches and pains, with overall poor health. Seldom do they realise that their bitterness is an acid that is eroding their own physical health.

Acid, or toxic thinking creates an acidic body.

Acidosis is the path to sickness.

For perfect health . . . think and choose Love!

March 25th

When we perceive life in a limited way, it is a reflection of our limits.

Every time we look at what we do not have, or cannot do, we are looking at our limits.

When we see what is wrong with the world, we have a focus on what is wrong with *our* personal world. Everything that we observe that is not as we think it should be is reflecting back to us what we see wrong in *our* life.

A child does not look at the world through the eyes of expectation or judgement; a child lives with, and experiences, its life in the moment.

Be like the child, open and innocent. Learn to swap *what should be* for *all that is now.* It will prove to be a very beneficial exchange!

And while you are at it . . . choose Love!

For as long as we need to understand Truth,
we never will.

To try to understand Truth is the same as putting yourself in prison, while Truth roams free. Understanding has a real place in the world of reason and logic – the intellectual world – but it has only a small part to play on your spiritual path.

Truth cannot be claimed by understanding, yet it can be fully embraced by *knowing*. For as long as you are attached to understanding you will never *know* Truth.

Replace the need to understand Truth with the ability to truly *trust* in Self.

Trust in Self accompanies . . . choosing Love!

March 27th

Inner knowing is the result of a focus on Truth;
asking no questions, seeking no answers,
needing no conclusions.

A non-intellectual focus on Truth becomes a direction in which your life will flow. Truth becomes a way of life, a path of Love.

At my Intensives I ask people to keep their questions to the last afternoon of the last day. Questions come from the intellect. I encourage the participants to involve their heart. There are no questions in the heart; this is the place of inner knowing.

Live with an open heart, and a sense of inquiry that has no questions, seeks no answers, and has no attachment to conclusions.

You will go far.

Divine discontent is often found in the search for spiritual Truth.

Divine discontent is an experience that many people encounter on their spiritual path. Some seekers change their path, not liking the feeling, believing that it indicates they are on the wrong path. This is not necessarily so.

What I call divine discontent is the experience of accepting nothing less than Truth. Self will never feel content with spiritual diatribe, only Love/Truth will truly feed the soul.

Divine discontent does not mean you must change your path, it mostly means that you are progressing well. Feed yourself positive energy by consciously . . . choosing Love!

March 29th

Today's greed cannot see tomorrow's need.

Greed is fear-based – the fear of not having enough. This fear has no caring for anything other than feeding its own rapacious appetite. The name of that appetite is greed.

Greed knows nothing of tomorrow's needs, nor does it care. If you are a person with greed, be careful not to feed it. Let it starve to death. If greed has a place in your life it is very much to your detriment.

Trust in today. You cannot have both trust and greed. Choose trust. Trust will take you beyond greed. So will . . . choosing Love!

Habit is given birth when we cling to the
decay of the moment.

The moment is ever-new – the continuity of now. Basically, this means that in-the-moment habit is impossible. To live this way would be a very high attainment. I have habits. With a single exception, they are ones that I enjoy.

What I refer to as the decay of the moment is brought about by spending the moment worrying about the future or the past.

As soon as worry begins its litany of fear, the newness of the moment is being eroded and your potential is being diminished.

This does not work for you! Be conscious, the one place where habits cannot dwell.

*The rare fruit of wisdom cannot be plucked
from the Tree of Life, nor can it in any way
be plundered.*

Every plant, from tiny moss to the largest tree, bears a harvest when it reaches the maturity of its growth. This is the natural way.

When animals reach maturity they breed, reproducing their own kind. They reach a time when they physically excel, then the process of decline begins.

So too, we reach a peak of physical maturity, but we have an extra gift: we can continue to grow in insight and intuition, in Love and self-acceptance, and in our pure joy of living life to the full richness of our Being. This is the way of spiritual alchemy. Only in this way do we experience the rare harvest of wisdom.

Spiritual alchemy is . . . choosing Love!

The thirty days of the month of

APRIL

Thought for the month:

Most people view life through the framework of separation, looking for conclusions and understanding.

Better to look at life as a continuous and on-going expression, looking through the eyes of acceptance at life's wondrous Mystery.

APRIL 1st

The simple power of a fool can be greater than the power of a king.

A king or queen is looked on as powerful, but this is only within society. Outside society a king or queen has no more power than any other person.

By contrast, the fool has already been cast out of society by a judgemental intellect that has found the fool to be too simple.

Within society, the throne of power is held by the intellect's reign of illusion.

Outside society, with simple vision, the fool recognises Truth. This is the power that enables the fool to embrace Self.

Never to be underestimated, simple is powerful.

So is . . . Love!

Before we can be truly mindful, we must become mindless. In this way the mind serves Self, rather than self serving the mind.

With the mind full of the detritus of life, it can literally ferment, causing a type of mental inebriation. This is the person who, addicted to thinking, is regurgitating continually their endless negative mental clutter.

When we surrender the mind, discarding our burden of thought, letting go all attachment to our thoughts, to the 'rights and wrongs' of the 'this and that' of life, we become mindless.

It is quite a paradox when you consider that we need to be mindless to be more mindful!

APRIL 3rd

Happiness is the passive state, and joy the active state of a positive consciousness.

While happiness is an emotion, joy is more. However, both are expressions of an inner state of consciousness. Being happy does not need a cause, it is a state of being.

Joy is the more active, dynamic expression of consciousness, yet it is probably less visible to other people than happiness.

Happiness easily writes its expression on the face, and is contagious, while joy, though quieter, is more powerful and transforming for it comes from deep within.

As happiness is to self . . . joy is to Self.

A trigger for joy is found by . . . choosing Love!

Depression is the passive state, and anger the active state of a negative consciousness.
(This does not apply to clinical depression).

Depression is probably the greatest health problem today. All stress related disease is the result of inner negativity.

Depression is a passive destroyer, gradually strangling all enthusiasm for life and living.

Depression looks at what is wrong with life, empowering the negativity that gave it birth.

Depression holds hands with stress, anxiety, isolation and suicide.

Anger is the active expression of the same negative consciousness. Anger explodes into the world around it, expelling the violence that has been brewing in the negative morass.

Developing an acceptance *of self*, rather than feeding the anger directed *at self*, is a positive way forward. I also recommend the constant and conscious practice of . . . choosing Love!

APRIL 5th

Uncertainty is a certain restriction!

Uncertainty is a limit. Let us look at 'uncertain' as 'indecisive,' and 'certain' as 'decisive'.

Being indecisive is based in a fear of making the wrong decision. This has its roots in doubt, meaning an old program of insecurity is firmly in place.

As crazy as it sounds, you cannot make a wrong decision. In the overall movie of your life, any decision will reap its own harvest of joy and sorrow. However, having said that, let me affirm that in the long term, decisions from the head will hold the most sorrow, while decisions from the heart will hold the most joy.

A heart decision is to always . . . choose Love!

*Living with courage means not being limited
by your fears.*

For most people, various fears are part of our everyday life. Some fears we can live with, some we can laugh at, some we can bypass, but our more powerful fears crack the whip that ruthlessly controls our lives.

Living with courage means acknowledging our fears, even accepting them, but not allowing the fears to limit, restrict, or contain our life.

It is a Truth that every fear is false.

If you face your fear, totally confronting it, you will find it is without any power. Fear is an impostor. Do not let fear indefinitely impose its false illusions over you. Choose Love!

APRIL 7th

Do 'now' . . . not worry how.

So many people procrastinate. They worry so much about the results of whatever it is that should be done, that they seldom ever get around to doing it. This is not a good way to live. Whatever it is that needs to be done, do it today. Not soon, or later, but . . . today.

Tomorrow never arrives!

The person who continually procrastinates will find that unnoticed, they put their whole life on hold. There comes a time when nothing in their life seems to be progressing, or moving forward.

Unrealised in the overall haste of life, all our procrastination, all our negative preoccupations, our reluctance to fully commit ourselves to life, reaps its own unwanted harvest.

Once again, consciously . . . choose Love!

Death is no more than a passage between visible and invisible realities.

Humanity has a very mixed relationship with death. Different religions encourage different beliefs, ranging from reincarnation, to residing in heaven, to death is the grand finale.

In Truth, there is no death. Death as we know it is the shedding of physicality, moving into our mostly unrealised metaphysical reality.

We can, in fact, while still physically alive travel into the metaphysical realms of so-called death, but there is a limit as to how far. For most people fear puts the lid on any such venture!

Death is a grand illusion. And a very disempowering one. A fixed belief in death will maintain and foster all too much unnecessary fear.

Jealousy is no more than a lack of self-confidence.
Jealousy acts as though Love is limited.

A person who has full confidence in Self does not suffer jealousy. Sometimes a sick child gets so much parental attention that the other siblings may get jealous. In children this is very understandable, in adults it remains childish.

A perceived lack of attention, or of Love, is the main reason for adult jealousy, indicating that the person concerned is rather immature.

For anyone suffering jealousy, it is wise to learn and *know* that Love is neither rationed nor limited.

Jealousy is an issue concerning deep emotional insecurity. You can assist in meeting your needs in this area by meeting the same needs in other people. As *you* learn to choose Love, so you will be guiding them in the same direction.

Passion is the 'fire in the forge'. This is the inner heat and power that transforms lives.

I have noticed that a lot of people are rather half-hearted about life. "Quite nice," sums it up. I have never been like that. I speak in terms of "Very nice," "Great," "Wonderful," Magnificent."

Just this morning, while talking to some gardeners about our recent, drought-breaking rain, they were most passionate about it.

And that is the key. Passion is the passport to a life of fulfilment and fun, to seeing all your dreams come true. Enthusiasm is the starting point of a rich and rewarding life, but it is passion that will empower the journey.

Passion for your life, for your spouse and family, even for work, and definitely for play, is the alchemy that takes you away from mediocrity and toward the magnificent.

Choosing Love is a fuel for your passion.

APRIL 11th

Freedom is not where you are, or even what you are doing; it is all based in your relationship with yourself.

You could be on an island paradise, with every luxury at your fingertips, every wish fulfilled, but even all this luxury has nothing to do with freedom. Most likely you would simply want more!

Freedom is truly based in your relationship with yourself. If you Love yourself, you could experience freedom in a prison cell. Your body can be confined, but not your spirit-Self; and freedom truly is a spiritual experience.

You can be free within duty to others, within a regular routine, within business, because true freedom is a within-self experience.

I also need to state that endless 'wants' curtail and limit any relationship with freedom.

Freedom is found by . . . choosing Love!

You are far, far greater than you ever dream or could ever imagine you are.

Overall, one of humanity's long-term problems is one of low self-esteem. Most people do not really like themselves. Few will admit this in public, most will acknowledge it deep inside. We act as though we are not good enough, yet nothing could be further from the Truth.

Each person is a magnificent, metaphysical, multidimensional, immortal Being of Love/Light. We are each Love and Light made manifest.

We have the gift of free will, meaning we can create and determine our own life/reality. Instead of continuing to create a mundane reality based in low self-esteem, create a reality that honours the magnificent Being you truly are.

Consciously . . . choose Love!

April 13th

It is a universal Truth that we each create our own life/reality, yet so few really know it. Of those few, even fewer live it.

In every moment of your life, you are creating the content and the direction of every moment of your life. This is the same statement, but it makes you think more deeply as you engage the words. You realise that your every thought and accompanying emotion – right now! – is creating the very substance of your life.

This is a very sobering realisation. It means that you cannot blame anybody for anything. And blame for many people is a full time occupation!

Once you grasp the reality of this, you realise that your life is yours to wonderfully create, or mess up!

Have I mentioned . . . choosing Love?!

In the bud of innocence awaits the bloom of Truth.

My favourite aphorism. It conjures up great beauty. We are all born with this Truth. It is part of our Being.

This Truth is not external to us, it is within. When we seek it we create the illusion that it is elsewhere; it is not. When we live from the heart/soul, we live in a place of innocence. There is no struggle, no failure or victories . . . we are at peace. A childlike state of innocence is often described today as being gullible, or naive, this is a cynical viewpoint. Be childlike, open and naive . . . experience the birth of your innocence.

In the fresh and open breeze of life, innocence and Truth hold hands.

I am naive and I . . . choose Love!

APRIL 15th

While Love is the master of Truth, fear is the master of illusion.

Human Love mostly expresses itself through the limits of our emotions. Yet Love is not an emotion. Although Love can never be limited, we most certainly limit our relationship with Love.

The most difficult expression of Love for us is truly to Love ourselves. This is unfortunate because it is only in our ability to Love ourselves that we find our deepest inner Truth.

Fear is a very old program in humanity. We created our fears long, long ago, and they are deeply installed in our conditioning. To this day fear weaves the same illusions, creating the same debilitating effect as of old.

The more you live in life's dynamic moment, the less the illusions of fear can overwhelm and limit you. Seriously . . . choose Love!

While Love expresses itself through open honesty, fear projects itself through deceit.

Love is the most open and honest expression that is possible. To Love another person is very normal, but to demonstrate that Love in everyday life is much less common. Love is like a fire, it needs constant fuel. A focus on Love in caring human relationships is the best of fuels to feed it.

Fear has no true reality. It is based in illusion and it specialises in deceit. It erodes your inner power reducing you in terms of energy. You are required to find the energy to create fear, and also to effectively maintain your relationship with it. This is known as long-term conditioning.

Fear has no real substance. Based in our deeply imprinted negative experiences of the past, it directs our negative thoughts of the moment into ever continuing repeats of the past. Thus illusions of being incapable and powerless continue; yet none of this is based in Love and Truth. It is in this way we give away our power.

Have I mentioned . . . choosing Love?!

APRIL 17th

Love is a freedom that cannot be denied, while fear holds you forever in denial.

When you are expressing unconditional Love you are touching the very fabric of life. When you are expressing unconditional Love, you are not only healing yourself, but, on a subtle level, you are also positively affecting all those whom you deeply Love.

Fear immobilises many people; they are frozen with fear. Yet, as I constantly teach, fear has no true reality, no true power.

To disarm any fear: Face it – Evaluate – Act – Relax. First, face the issue. Next evaluate how to act in a way that can free you to fearlessly choose. Then act on this.

Finally, just let it go. Relax, and . . . choose Love!

By not choosing Love, people inadvertently choose
fear. In other words, by not choosing Love, all
unrealised, the habit of fear chooses us.
A dangerous habit!

We should not need to choose Love – we are
designed to express it naturally – yet Love
now has to be a conscious choice.

If we choose Love consciously at times that could
be very stressful, we empower ourselves. Equally, if
we choose Love instead of reacting negatively and
fearfully, we empower ourselves.

If we do not choose Love, fear is waiting in our
subconscious program ready to sabotage us.

By not choosing Love consciously, we are at the
mercy of our subconscious fears. And fear has no
mercy.

Begin today by consciously . . . choosing Love. But
always remember, you can only choose Love by
consciously living it.

Wholeness is a reality revealed by Love, while separation is a concept sustained by ignorance.

How odd. We live in a world of interconnection, all life expressing One consciousness in a vast diversity; all life One holistic expression. Despite this, the basic human experience is one of separation.

We look across the distance between our bodies and we believe that physical apartness means that we are each separate from all other people and Nature. This illusion is what we believe and live.

People ignore their inner Truth because the intellect denies a holistic reality. The intellect accepts that if enough people believe in an unrealised error . . . by the power of numbers it must be true. This creates an all-too-common consensual error!

If you accept that you are Lovingly connected to all life, you are on the path to experiencing wholeness.

Freedom is not found in being perfect, it is found in being perfectly free.

Many people believe that God is perfect, and by implication, we are therefore imperfect. Some religions revile our so-called imperfections, making a tenet of it. A deeper, non-religious Truth reveals that God created perfectly, so the whole concept of humanity being fundamentally imperfect, is flawed.

For humanity to be perfect does not mean that we always behave perfectly; far from it. It is about giving our best when it is required. It is about being free enough to consciously . . . choose Love!

If, however, you are unsure about all this, just release the whole concept of perfection.

You can more easily act and be perfectly free without trying to understand the perfection of imperfections!

"I can't afford" is a common expression.
You cannot afford for exactly as long as
you believe you cannot afford.

Our thoughts and beliefs create our reality. One of the most common is the "I can't afford"syndrome. As stated in my aphorism, for as long as you believe this, you are right.

Remove yourself from gazing at, and wanting things that obviously, you cannot afford. Begin to think and act within your financial means, so you can stop saying, "I can't afford."

The constant repetition of this negative little comment is very powerful. It creates a focus in your life that will detain you within the prison of fear and financial hardship.

Once you terminate this negative bias, you may be surprised at how many opportunities come your way that can solve your financial problems.

Everything is a reflection of perfection. Dismiss the imperfection of the reflection, and focus only on the perfection.

There are two ways of seeing life: one is to see it the way it appears to be, the other is to see it through the eyes of perfection.

You cannot force the latter. Where I once saw what was wrong in life, I now see the perfection. Where I once looked through the limited eyes of blame and adverse judgement, I now see through the eyes of Love and acceptance.

Life is not the way that it appears to be. The poor beggar may well be richer than the wealthy man, while a person dying may finally be finding life.

You also find life by consciously . . . choosing Love!

APRIL 23rd

While the intellect will never experience wholeness, intelligence will never know separation.

In the world today, people worship at the altar of the intellect. This is unfortunate.

The intellect likes to demonstrate just how clever it is, never realising that cleverness can all too often be the twin of stupidity.

The intellect relates to all life as separate; this illusion is the breeding place of prejudice.

Intelligence relates to all life in a holistic way, knowing that everything in life is connected.

Every one of us has the choice of whether to relate to life through our intellect/brain, or our intelligence/heart.

*Without effort you can maintain the adverse situation
you are in; changing it requires effort. You change it
by knowing that you are not the situation.*

All too easily people get caught up in
everyday problems: financial struggles,
emotional upsets, or just depressed and unhappy.
Consequently they think and speak in terms of,
"I never have enough money," or, "I am full of fear
and anxiety," or, "I am sick." Not a good idea!

By doing this, we strongly identify ourselves with
our problem. We make it personal. We claim and
own it, literally stating in consciousness that I am
this problem, or sickness. This is a huge error.

You are not the problem. To be accurate, you are
a magnificent human Being who is denying their
magnificence and claiming sickness or misery.

Be very careful; what you continually affirm in
consciousness will eventually become your reality.

Better by far to affirm your Truth by constantly and
consciously . . . choosing Love!

April 25th

Focus on the target, but 'live' the arrow in flight.

Suppose you have a business ambition, or a wish to be spiritually enlightened, or whatever your target is that you are aiming at.

Focus on that target clearly, without seeing any problems or difficulties. This clears the way. Seeing problems creates obstructions.

You must now bring your awareness and full expression into the moment. You know the target, it is in your focus, now . . . you live as the arrow in flight. The more focussed and clear your vision, the truer and more sure flies your arrow-self.

Unconditional Trust is the flight of the arrow.

Light is the illumination of eternity.

There are physical laws on this planet, even if more subtle than yet realised. But life is first and foremost a metaphysical expression, just as first and foremost we are metaphysical Beings. In this Greater Reality, light is not experienced in the same way as a physical reality.

Rather than light travelling at 5000 kilometres per second, light is the substance of so-called space. When I say light is the illumination of eternity, I do not mean sunlight, moonlight, or light from any physical source; I mean the true Love/Light of Creation.

You do not end a belief by not believing it, you end it by not living it.

No longer believing something that for a long time has been a fixed belief, changes nothing.

Once that belief program is set in place, it is no mere mental belief; it is an established way of living your life and expressing yourself.

To end a belief that negatively affects your life you are required to stop living that outmoded belief. It works best by replacing the old belief with another, more supportive one, and living it.

Note that *living it* is the key ingredient. This requires continual conscious attention.

Believe that you will gain your spiritual freedom by consciously . . . choosing Love!

There are fish that swim and live on the surface of the pond, and others which live in the depths.

Fish follow their own biological program for survival, finding their niche in the great oceanic 'pond' of fishy life.

We are not fish! Neither are we here on Earth simply to survive, or create wealth. We are here to consciously discover and live the creative principles of human life. When we learn that Love is the path to wholeness, we have found the path of harmony and balance.

But like fish, there are the people who live on the very surface of life, skimming along in their daily living in a way that never allows them to plumb the depths of life, or to ponder the greater Mystery that surrounds them.

Equally, there are those who live submerged in the greater depths, their lives dedicated to the spiritual revelations that this mode of life reveals.

There are no wrongs or rights to any of this, just our differences.

April 29th

You were born to fly on the wings of Love. If you want to fly, then mix with those few people who know Self, and are already flying high.

People are inclined to make heavy work out of life. I know I once did. But this is not the way it has to be. Let go of the foolish 'Life was not meant to be easy' syndrome, and step far more lightly. Easy or difficult, life is as you make it.

If you want to fly on the uplifting thermals of Love, you need to look for other people who are already doing this. And there are such people.

Mix with the positive people, the ones who are Love-hearted, who see the beauty in life, and who take full responsibility for themselves.

These people are the best flight attendants you will ever get!

If you want to fly with eagles, mix with eagles.

There are many people in life who aspire to greatness in sport, business, the arts: the list is long. And this is to be applauded.

There are also those fewer people in life who aspire to live their spiritual greatness.

These are the eagles. They fly on the high thermals of Love, and from their higher perspective they see the picture of life on a much greater canvas than those people whose vision has never been elevated. The higher they fly, the more they live beyond the sight of the consensus public.

You create uplifting thermals by constantly and consciously . . . choosing Love!

The thirty-one days of the month of

MAY

Thought for the month:

Most people live a life of wants, never realising that desire is the foundation of wanting. The more we feed our wants in a fruitless search for happiness, the more desire and wants control our life.

Better to see life in the unfolding fortunes of the moment, knowing that that which is needed will duly manifest itself, while that which is wanted continues to reflect the desires of the mind.

MAY 1st

To be lost in thought is to lose the moment.

So many people spend much of their lives literally lost in thought. It reminds me of the old TV series, Lost in Space. No difference!

You can think your way out of the moment, but you cannot think your way into it. Think about this when you are not thinking!

Herein lies the whole basis for meditation.

When you bring your attention to experiencing fully the *doing* and *being* of the moment, you will find that thought becomes less dominant.

It is the Now moment that offers all the fruits of life.

Consciously choosing Love is a rich fruit indeed.

Separation seeks to fix and make rigid; movement is flexibility and connection, a denial of separation. Fixed belief is an expression of separation.

The experiences of your everyday life are usually seen through the eyes of separation. You need to remember that separation and illusion go hand-in-hand.

When you fix your beliefs, and thoughts follow along fixed and stuck parameters, then your life is in a rut. Be open and flexible in all aspects of life.

Do not be too eager to build structures of limitation into your life.

Use all the time you need to see and take a more holistic and connected direction.

Nothing creates a more holistic and connected direction than consciously . . . choosing Love!

MAY 3rd

The price you pay for being great is to think great thoughts and speak great words about yourself.

The most perfect example of this was the boxer, Mohammed Ali. He always referred to himself as the 'greatest', and if heavyweight boxing was his proving ground, he probably was.

There was a price. The media gave him hell. He was called arrogant, bigheaded, vain and conceited, yet through it all he continued to say and think, 'I am the greatest.'

Do not be afraid to pay the price for speaking your worth 'up' in the world. You have already spent far to long speaking yourself down.

For me, claiming my greatness was my most difficult challenge. But no longer – I am GREAT!

Remember, you can speak yourself 'up' only if you are thinking yourself 'up'.

*No form of work is unworthy, but doing what
you truly dislike on a daily basis is a form of
self-punishment. This is unworthy of you.*

If you are going to work each day to do something
that you really dislike simply for the money, you
are living in a manner that is unworthy of you. This
means living in the 'hate Monday, hurry up Friday'
syndrome.

What a punishing way to live!

If you believe that you have no skills and no choice,
then you are right, but only because you believe it
and thus create it.

If you believe that you deserve better, and that you
deserve work that you enjoy doing, work that is
worthy of you, then this also can be your reality.

However, don't wait for it to happen, make it
happen! It is your reality, your life.

Make it happen by . . . choosing Love!

May 5th

Reality is not the event, but your experience and memory of it.

M ost people believe that all reality is the same. This is not true. Every person on this planet experiences their own personal reality, but we do have huge areas where we are all basically in agreement. We call this a consensus reality: a reality of all agreeing to the same illusion!

Each nation has its own consensus reality. It is obvious that an Arab consensus reality is very different from an American consensus reality, but even these have their overlap of agreement.

In the end, however, reality is not what is happening around you, it is your experience and perception of it. In other words, for each of us, our reality is unique. Most arguments arise from one person attempting to impose their reality on other people. Pure ignorance!

Every judgement you make of yourself will always prove to be unworthy of you.

Only when you live without judgement will you know peace, and only when all judgement of yourself ceases will you find yourself worthy.

Avoid all judgement. Judging the world, its people, your relatives, the 'them and theys', the movers and shakers, the multinationals, is just so much wasted energy. There is nothing that is honouring in making judgements. By far the better way is to discern in how you live your life. Discernment denotes intelligence; judgment is the path of the intellect.

Give your attention to the beauty of life. See the sparkle of newness in the day and share it with a smile. For yourself . . . choose Love!

MAY 7th

Our birthright is so much greater than we ever allow ourselves to receive.

It is the birthright of every person to live in the Golden Castle of Abundance on the peaks of the Mountains of Beauty. Why then, do we settle for so much less?

Rather than see ourselves as magnificent and ultra-worthwhile, far too many people view themselves as unworthy and unlovable.

Mediocrity is a program of conditioning. While golden castles and the like are just metaphors, we are real. Our suffering is real in the midst of harmony, humanity's steadily increasing poverty is real in the midst of abundance.

It does not have to be this way!

Change the program. Choose Love!

Cast your sights high and the spirit soars,
cast your sights low and the spirit falls.

Far too many people look at life through the eyes of pessimism. They believe that life is too good to be true, so they harvest all that is false. They become cynical, and their spirits plummet. Not a good way to live!

If you look to life through optimistic eyes you may occasionally be disappointed. This means that you keep the optimism flowing, and you continue to keep your sights high, open to the uplifting sunshine of life.

Live in it, bathe in it, excel in it. Your spirit will soar, and your optimism will reward you, for you are the creator of your life. Again . . . choose Love!

May 9th

Honour self by being true to Self – always.

To be true to yourself means to honour Self always. Self is who you are, a magnificent Being of Love and Light. Living this is living your very highest value, living your true worth.

There are so many moments in life when you can be very much less. It is so easy. Too much to drink: foolishly saying 'yes' when 'no' would be so much smarter: shoplifting little items because they are of low value: telling lies about other people. There are hundreds of daily ways to demean and cheapen yourself.

None of this implies that you are bad or wicked, but it is a way of dishonouring Self, which, in turn, will reduce the quality of your life.

If you are generous to people, life will be generous to you.

There are two basic types of giving. One is giving from the true generosity of spirit, the other is more about giving from an act of conscience during global or local disasters, and to disadvantaged people in need.

Generosity of spirit usually involves the giving of yourself, while giving where there is need usually takes the form of money or gifts.

Please note that there is no right or wrong in any of this. No matter how you give, if your generosity and giving comes truly from the heart, there is no difference in either form of giving.

I would add that it is wise not to neglect also being generous of spirit in giving to yourself. A perfect example is the act of . . . choosing Love!

MAY 11th

Consensus illusion will always be uncomfortable,
for it is made from the fabric of deceit.

Consensus reality is no more than an overall human agreement about the illusions of life. The deeper a person's involvement in this mass illusion, the more discomfort will be in their life.

There is no hiding place from this. Some people seek to hide behind wealth, but discomfort will be firmly entrenched, perhaps in the guise of poor, and deteriorating health or relationships.

To any enquiring human intelligence, it is blindingly obvious that life has many anomalies.

Why not look deeper, seeking the Truth of life? Anything that does not fully embrace Truth is spun from the lies of deceit. Be aware that we are living in times when the controlling cartels will do their best to ensnare and entangle you in their lies, deceit, and their carefully crafted illusions.

You may well disapprove, but do not get attached to your disapproval.

I t is perfectly acceptable to disapprove of something, but be sure not to dwell on that disapproval. Once you become fixated on what it is that you disapprove of, you will attract more and more into your life which merits your disapproval.

There are certain things that I disapprove of – child pornography on the internet is one of them – but I have never even looked at it.

I leave it out of my conscious focus, and it never intrudes. I know it is there and I find it a disgusting violation. End of story.

When you get angry over something of which you disapprove, but take no action to end its existence, you simply give it your power.

Constructively oppose it, or . . . choose Love!

May 13th

*If you do not understand, then your lack of
understanding is revealing the nature of the
handicap . . . the need to understand.*

When I talk of this in my Intensives, people
really struggle with the idea of not needing
to understand. The need to understand your
spiritual Self is a powerful handicap, simply
because such an understanding attempts to reduce
the unknown to the known. A path into Mystery
cannot be intellectually known!

Truly, life is about Mystery. Do you not see that you
can move with intelligence much further into the
Mystery of life than you can when restricted by the
limits and dogma of the intellect?

This is so clear and obvious.

If you travel your spiritual path with intellect,
you have to lead it by the hand, for it is severely
handicapped. If you travel with intelligence, you
are guided and nurtured all the way.

Intelligence . . . chooses Love!

The need to understand is an intellectual habit.
Understanding is always based in the past or future,
while Truth resides only in the moment.

Everything I ever needed to know about life
I learned after I left school. The only thing I
learned of real benefit at school was reading. Once
I discovered the joy of books, I found my way out of
the school's intellectual clutch.

I left school before I was fifteen, my intellect never
stimulated overmuch. When I needed a day off
school, intelligence offered a way out.

Now, as I look back, the way out was, in fact, my
way in.

School tried to teach me that life is no more than
an intellectual exercise. I have since learned that
life is the expression of the moment, experienced
within a framework of conscious intelligence.

But then, how could school teach what it had not
yet learned? Nobody ever taught the teachers the
wisdom of . . . choosing Love!

May 15th

Be aware that you are always creating your own reality, even when you are not aware of it. Like . . . now!

Every moment of our lives we are creating our own reality. We don't even have time off for a coffee. Reality rules, okay!

If you were to observe some of your less than memorable moments, times when you have handled life rather badly, you would realise that throughout all those episodes you were creating your own reality. There is no time out.

Conversely, times when you are really proud of yourself, moments when you know that you have got it all together, these too are you creating your own reality.

To create a life of abundance and joy takes less effort than to create a life of mishap and mayhem. All you need do is simply . . . choose Love!

Who you are is One with All that Is. In other words, 'There is nothing outside Self.'
This is the expression of a Greater Reality.

The framework of aware consciousness that expresses itself into, and beyond the physical body as we know it, is Self.

There are no borders and boundaries to the consciousness of Self, because consciousness expresses wholeness. Note that wholeness is not the sum of separation.

The consciousness of Self is One with All. To be spiritually enlightened is simply an essence of living within this experience.

There is nothing outside Self. Think about this for a few moments. Try to grasp the immense implications of it, and then consider how it fits in with consensus reality.

It does not!

Adverse judgement and blame were not born from intelligence. They are the spawn of separation, and are expressed by the intellect. Their expression consumes your energy, with debilitating effect.

A belief in separation gives birth to fear and isolation. From this potent inner brew negative judgements and blame draw their required energy. Note that blaming people consumes much basic energy. The more you blame and judge, the greater your fatigue and illnesses will become. Intelligence does not judge, neither does it compare, or blame.

The intellect requires you to constantly feed it energy, while intelligence is constantly energising you. Life is as it is. Realise that all our negative judging and blaming changes nothing, other than to negate the energy of our own lives. To attain a constant supply of energy . . . choose Love!

*Pain and suffering are a measure of your resistance
to change.*

S o many people who are in a major life crisis
suddenly fall seriously ill. A crisis in life is a
strong message to make major changes in your
lifestyle, in your thinking, in your attitude, or in all
of these, and more.

A serious health crisis is a signal that you are
resisting change and inner growth in your life.
A heart attack is a very powerful way of saying
that you have bypassed your heart in your whole
approach to life. Now, suddenly, a heart bypass is
looming. Move and flex with change. Change is a
regular feature in life, so you may as well learn to
go with it, rather than resist it.

You more easily embrace change by constantly and
consciously . . . choosing Love!

MAY 19th

You truly Change yourself by knowing and living Truth. Truth . . . Self is perfect and there is nothing to deliberately change.

I am referring to Change here at a far higher, more spiritual level. When you know and live the Truth of Self, this is reflected into the life of identity-self. By doing this there is nothing to change, for your focus and, to the best of your ability, your expression, is based in Self.

Never dwell on anything negative you think you may need to change in yourself. Wallowing in the negative defeats the purpose.

Give thought instead to everything you approve of in yourself, giving these positive assets the benefit of your energy.

Change is both subtle and dynamic. A sensible way to create change is by . . . choosing Love!

In Truth, a near-death experience is more often than not, a near-life experience.

Most people go through their lives so deeply embedded in illusion that they never even get close to the Truth of life. Being alive is not necessarily indicative of life being lived in a fulfilling or creative way.

Your life always moves toward your focus, becoming your life experience. If your goal does not embrace Truth, you are less likely to have an in-depth experience of life.

Occasionally, however, when a dying, or very badly injured person is relaxed, and the fight for life finished, the illusion wavers, and they have a close up real-life encounter. What a gift!

MAY 21st

The furthest away you can ever be from spiritual enlightenment is also the closest you can get.

I have had people say to me at Intensives that they feel so very far away from a state of enlightenment. When I ask why they feel this way, they generally tell me that for them, enlightenment is a huge journey that is so far removed from their lives as to be impossible.

These people are regarding spiritual enlightenment as some unlikely, and very distant event.

You need to realise that spiritual enlightenment is not a distant event – unless you believe it is!

Instead of a distant view, do a complete about turn, and look deeply into yourself . . . with Love.

Love . . . it is that close!

Attachment is the denial of our expansion, change, and inner growth.

Our life is all about change. Change leads to expansion and growth.

A seedling tree is in a constant state of change as it grows, its expansion tremendous. Compare a mature tree trunk with the stem of a sapling. Unlike us, Nature is open to this natural progression in all its many diverse forms.

When it comes to humanity, change is both resisted and feared. Cultures cling tenaciously to their everyday rituals, fearing change. If you have this fear attachment, you should be aware that your future will continue to be more of your recycled past.

Let go of all emotional attachments, and with courage, accept change as a permanent and very necessary aspect of your life. Even attract change by . . . choosing Love!

MAY 23rd

Self-empowerment is about putting positive action to positive thought.

There are many people who engage in positive thinking, yet their lives are still not to their liking, never quite reaching their expectations.

When this point is made to me, I mostly ask them if they have put all this positive thought into action.

Some people look startled with the suggestion. It seems they had learned that a positive life is all about positive thinking – that's it. They were waiting for the benefits.

Live your positive thinking; activate it, make it real, fully engage life, then the benefits will flow.

Remember, you are the creator of the content and the direction of your life. Always . . . choose Love!

What the head ponders, the heart knows.

Obviously I am a heart person. This is not the emotional centre, it is the intelligence centre.

I meet so many people who struggle to get an intellectual grip on what I talk about. Yet when, after a couple of days at an Intensive, they escape from the 'brain' domination, it all just unfolds into their awareness, and they are so surprised at how easy it is.

If you are a brain person, give it a rest. Pay your heart a visit and you may stay awhile. Have a friendly chat about your magnificent Self! Communication is not exclusive to the head. The heart both transmits and receives pure, wise, intelligent, communication. It is the heart that consciously . . . chooses Love!

MAY 25th

Reality and illusion both occupy the same space.

When the majority of your reality is made up of illusion – convincing and powerful as it may be, it is still illusion – it is not easy to let go.

You do not even know what to release, and many of your friends will think you are mad if you try to talk about it.

Reality and illusion occupy the same space, but there is no conflict between them.

Illusion is the mind's fabrication of your beliefs, conditioning, and attachments, while reality is the result of your heart embracing life's Mystery.

You need not try to understand reality; a deep and abiding trust in yourself will reveal it.

Unconditional Love is the death of illusion.

Nobody comes to know the Truth of Self without courage and commitment.

I mention Truth and Self a great deal. I have no choice if I am to serve you truly through this book! It is about Truth/Love and Self, and life as it IS. Truth/Love and Self are the substance of your Being.

This not something that you have to learn, only to *be*. You cannot fake it!

To reach into the Truth of Self does require a deep soul commitment. Of this, there is no doubt. And that commitment – which is going to change your whole life – requires courage.

The courage to release everything that holds you and binds you, everything that you most want and desire. Be aware, however, that releasing it does not necessarily mean that you have to lose it.

May 27th

There is no such thing as a so-called accident.
All accidents are unresolved purpose. Resolve the
purpose, and life will be the expression of purpose
without pain and suffering.

To believe in so-called accidents you have to believe in chance and separation – all illusion.

As a Being who has lived many lifetimes, you build up a lot of unresolved issues. This could be seen as karma, but I am giving you a more clear, if brief, definition.

An accident is Self bringing an unresolved issue back into your life and to your attention. Generally, ignorance continues, and the purpose behind the accident fails to be recognised.

Sometimes, however, people deal with their *accident-on-purpose* so well that the hidden and unresolved issue is brought to their awareness and finally dealt with. This will definitely decrease the recycling of so-called accidents. Also, by choosing Love you will decrease accidents.

What do you want in life? More of what you have been, or some of what you could be?

As we go through frame after frame of the movie, 'The Continuity of Self', we all develop certain skills. Generally, we tend to revisit and redevelop these skills lifetime after lifetime, enjoying the unrealised ease of this habitual learning. There is nothing wrong with this, but neither is it in our best interests.

Some *aware* people experience that 'I have done this before' feeling. Surprise!! If this is you, I recommend that you resist the temptation to follow the easier path of more-of-the-same, and learn new skills that will stretch and challenge you.

Generally speaking, the easy familiar path is no longer the most spiritually creative path for inner growth as a human Being in this present incarnation. Like elastic, we all need to be continually stretched.

MAY 29th

You always get exactly what you deserve, even if you think you do not always deserve what you get!

It is Self who decides what you get in life, even if identity-self does not understand how or why.

Self always brings into your life exactly what you deserve in the most appropriate timing. This does not mean you do not have free will to pick and choose, but as your relationship with Self becomes more conscious, more aware, so this 'deserve' factor is ever more invoked.

Of course, it can be very unpleasant, but so also conversely, it can be fantastic.

I have a wonderful marriage to my beautiful, Carolyn, so I obviously deserve her in my life. She also deserves me! We . . . chose Love!

Blame is a negative expression of reaction.

When we react against a person or situation, the first reaction is to blame. Newspapers often headline the words, WHO IS TO BLAME?

Why look to blame? Why not look at what has happened more creatively and without a blame attitude?

All that the search for blame achieves is bad feeling, anger, and festering resentment. As a reaction, blame never achieves anything. If a serious crime is committed, of course the police should look for the culprit, but I'm talking about our daily living type of blame.

Instead of blaming, attempt to see that what has taken place has an 'up' side as well as a 'down' side. A positive response is far more to your advantage than a negative reaction. Instead of blaming, a wise and positive response would be to consciously . . . choose Love!

Reaction is the abdication of choice.

How many people first react violently or with anger, and then regret it? I imagine that daily it must run into thousands of millions.

A reaction always comes from the past, from old patterns of negative behaviour. The person who lives their life continually reacting is the classic victim. They live on the 'down' side of life. They are stressed and depressed. When you react without thought or care, you have forsaken all choice regarding your life. You are creating a victim status for yourself.

When something or someone hits your reaction button, take a deep breath . . . and hold it. Hold it and keep on holding it. Finally, when you must, let the breath out slowly, and let your conditioned negative reaction depart with it.

Then, as positively as you can, deal with the person or situation. And consciously . . . choose Love!

The thirty days of the month of

JUNE

Thought for the month:

Most people talk of 'my 'mind and 'your' mind,
believing mind to be owned by each person.
These are the people who attempt to change
'your' mind if you are not in agreement with them.

Better to realise that all mind is One, and that
any strong fixation you have might eventually
become the fixation of some other person. The
reverse is also true!

June 1st

All time occupies the same space.

In our biological, 3-dimensional reality our whole physical existence is dominated and ruled by linear time.

There is also what I call a *spherical time frame.* This measures time in a metaphysical reality, but not in the way in which we relate to time. More simply put, in a greater reality all time occupies the same moment. Thus everything is happening in a simultaneous juxtaposition; meaning that the past and future occupy the present moment of life.

Your life as a physical person is ruled by linear time, but as a spiritual, or metaphysical Being, you live in a spherical time frame reality.

It is quite a task to bring these realities into a balance within ourselves! Interestingly enough, this is easily done by . . . choosing Love!

A low income early in life has a lot to teach,
so long as it does not teach you to remain
on a low income.

Starting your life on a high income may seem desirable, but it can teach you many undesirable habits. 'Easy come, easy go' is an old saying that carries a deal of truth. This is the place where extravagance has its roots, where lavish spending can lead you to later downfall.

If you start your working life on a low income, it helps trim your desire for every latest fashion or car, and it helps to build character. It also builds a compassion in you for those who remain on a low income. You learn that a person's worth has nothing to do with money.

However, do not let it teach you that you have no choice but to remain on a low income. If you follow your true passion in life, you will live with enthusiasm and prosperity will be a spin-off.

Enthusiasm and prosperity both . . . choose Love!

JUNE 3rd

Truth denies and defies the ordinary. Live Truth and you are extraordinary.

It is much easier to talk about Truth than it is to live it. Spirituality is often discussed, thereby creating much argument, but essentially, your spirituality is a way of life.

It is about living your physical life with a focus and awareness that you are a spiritual Being, and integrating this Truth into your daily life in whatever way is meaningful and real for you. Your way might be a completely different way from friends, or family; this is where dispute and argument is so easily born.

Live your view of Truth in the way that is true for you. It is not something to discuss or argue about; it is just a matter of living *your* spiritual life *your* own way, following *your* heart. By doing this you are no longer ordinary. Add to this consciously choosing Love on a daily basis, and you are truly extraordinary.

Every time you criticise yourself, you further reduce and limit your reality. This is reality diminished, the fabric of consensus reality.

Constant, repetitive criticism is an insidious erosion of your life. It is repetitive criticism that will shape your reality, not the occasional, discontent criticism. Consensus reality is made up of people in a fairly constant state of negative criticism, all coming from their deep subconscious.

This shapes people's lives, limiting them to a huge degree, even though such knowledge seems to be outside the awareness of most people.

Let go of continual self-criticism, and while you are at it, let go of *all* criticism. In this way you put aside your own limits and boundaries.

Instead of repetitive criticism, it would be wise to repetitively . . . choose Love!

Your life will be much lighter and happier.

June 5th

Self – who you are – expresses only from and within a Greater Reality.

Identity-self expresses mostly itself within the daily reality of illusion. The more limited your view of life, the more attached and dogmatic you are, the more powerful the illusion. This means the more powerfully it will hold and bind you.

Self, the immortal Being you truly are, lives only in a greater reality, a place of vitality and joy, of holistic interconnectedness, of Love and Light.

This can, of course, be your everyday reality. To choose it, you are required to *live* the choice. It helps enormously to . . . choose Love!

Self-denial propagates limitation.

When we propagate plants and seedlings, we have to be aware of the tiny new weeds that will also flourish and grow. In time, the difference between the wanted and unwanted will be clear.

Equally, in our daily lives we need to know the difference between the thoughts and beliefs that will assist us to grow strong and true, and the thoughts that, like weeds, will choke, stunt, and suppress our inner growth.

Self-denial is a very common weed in the garden of humanity. "I can't" or "I'm not clever enough," are weeds that impede far too many people.

Replace those thoughts with, "I am getting better every day." And repeat them out aloud whenever anyone asks you how you are. It works!

JUNE 7th

By believing in separation we create and experience isolation and loneliness.

All life is One. I have written this many times. It takes repetition for a Truth that is not easily accepted in life to really to sink in. The intellect can understand the words, but is unable to experience the meaning. This requires a more balanced whole-brain approach.

If we fully embrace and live this holistic Truth – we are all connected by consciousness – we will eventually holistically experience this deep inner connection.

However, this is not the way of consensus reality. While we continue to believe in separation, so we will experience and harvest our belief: isolation and loneliness. This false belief kills the elderly, alienates the young, and leads to both intercultural and personal conflict.

A path to experiencing Oneness is found by being conscious and . . . choosing Love!

By consciously living Oneness as best we can,
we may experience the connectivity of all life.

There is no technique or route I can offer that will allow you to experience Oneness. It does not happen like that. Oneness is a way of being, an inner knowing that gradually unfolds from within.

If you have a garden, you probably go out and spend time in it. If you see all life as separate while you work in your garden, you are *doing to* the garden. You may be a good gardener, but you are missing a vital connection.

By being aware of the Oneness in all life, and developing this, everything changes. Now, while you work in the garden, you are *being with* the garden and plants while you are working with them.

You are now making a connecting to the garden in a consciously aware, more transcendent way. If you also apply this to daily life, you are on a path to Oneness.

JUNE 9th

Separation is a habit; Oneness is a choice.

Separation is such an established habit it has become a permanent reality in the lives of most people. Separation is now such a stubborn, unyielding human condition that the doors of free choice are practically closed. So much so, that even to talk to consensus reality people of the greater reality of Oneness is to invite ridicule.

To experience Oneness you must consciously choose it. You make that choice by being conscious of your spiritual connection with all life. You choose by taking full responsibility for your own life, without blame, without criticism . . . and with appreciation.

Try it. With enough attention and persistence, one day the doors will creakingly begin to open . . . and the bright Light of Oneness will shine in.

You are then able to consciously . . . choose Love!

All life is absolute continuity and connection.

A bsolute means total, beyond all doubt.
This aphorism may, for you, carry some doubt.
It may be a concept for you, or just plain wrong,
but for me it is absolute.

If you cross the ocean in a ship, you will be aware
that beneath the surface is the true, unseen
vastness of the ocean. The ship merely engages the
surface.

Humanity is the ship on the vast ocean of life. The
way life is lived by the majority of people is to no
more than skim the surface of the ocean.

Deeper, much deeper, a vast, unfaltering current
carries our continuity connection to all life.

JUNE 11th

Your relationship with yourself is your relationship with life, and it is life's relationship with you.

If you have a negative relationship with yourself – and billions do – then you will have an equally negative relationship with life.

Life is not an outside Self event; nor is life confined by Nature or humanity, or by any physical bodies. The relationship you have with you, 'yourself' is your whole relationship with life, and it is life's relationship with you.

If you have a good relationship with yourself, you will be aware that life is also treating you kindly.

It cannot be overstated that your Loving relationship with yourself is also your relationship with abundance, with your health, with your family and other people.

An appreciative and Loving relationship with yourself is, literally, the key to liberating your life.

The key is to consciously . . . choose Love!

Judge little, but be very discerning.

Let me put this humorously: A man calls in at a motel for the night. He has his dinner, and is on his way back to his room, when he is waylaid by a very sexy woman. "We need one more man," she says, "will you join us?"

Looking into her room, the man sees a few people involved in group sex. If he says, "No way! What you are doing is wrong," he has been judgemental.

If he says, "Thanks for the offer, but that's not for me," he has been discerning.

If he joins in with their group sex, he has been neither judgemental nor discerning!

Do not be judgemental. Discernment is far more appropriate.

JUNE 13th

You cannot liberate the past if you cannot liberate the present.

I t is possible to change the past, but this is not the format for such an explanation. However, you cannot change or liberate the past if you do not have a dynamic interaction with life in the present moment.

All life is held in the moment: this is the key to changing the past. Anything in the past that is unresolved is unresolved now. To liberate the now-moment requires that you live within it.

It is surprising how very few people have any ability to consciously be in the moment. Living with your thoughts always adrift creates confusion. In no way can this facilitate supportive thoughts or positive action.

This is why I suggest . . . choosing Love!

Intellect conceptualises whilst intelligence 'knows'.
Trust your intuitive intelligence simply by living
your trust.

D o you trust the inner intelligence that speaks in a soft voice, and is invariably right? I doubt it. Yet this is the voice of intuition.

Generally we connect with our intuitive knowing, then we intellectualise it. We apply ever more logic and reason, regurgitating it over and over until the precious gem of *knowing* is lost in the confusion of thoughts. That moment of brief intuitive clarity has been irrevocably lost.

The path out of this common mess is to trust your inner knowing. Basically, this is no more than trusting the intelligence of Self, but people seldom regard it this way.

If you trust your intuitive intelligence you are building a more powerful, inner expression of intuitive intelligence to trust. As logic and reason is to the brain, so is intuitive intelligence to the heart.

Intuitive intelligence chooses Love!

JUNE 15th

Most people have a negative reaction when their reality is threatened. But a threatened reality is often the only way out.

If your reality is a consensus reality, there is not much chance of you changing it. By its very nature, a consensus reality clings to a copycat version of what it perceives in other similar people. This happens, even if you do not like it, or them!

One way out of this restricted reality is to have it severely threatened; this shocks and confronts a person, often forcing real change.

Do not avoid situations that threaten your status quo. Be aware that if your reality is so threatened that it feels as though it may collapse, unrealised by you, this confrontation will almost certainly have been self-invoked for your own benefit.

Let your tightly held reality collapse. Advance another step closer to your own eventual freedom.

Step by step . . . choose Love

With openness and acceptance comes expansion of consciousness.

How much easier it is to live with an open attitude, an open heart, and an open acceptance of life.

Why is it that most people live an almost opposite way? Closed and fixed beliefs and attitudes, rigid concepts of right and wrong, heavily critical, and their poor hearts struggling to keep beating.

To experience your full potential, you need to live with expansion as your constant companion. And I don't mean your waistline! You need to grow in consciousness, for this is the only measure of human growth and worth.

Openness and acceptance creates an energy that makes life easier and smoother. This does not mean that everything happens the way you *want* it, but almost invariably it will happen in the way that you *need* it.

When you accept life *as is*, you are growing toward your most perfect expression.

JUNE 17th

Pain and exhaustion erases resistance to change,
but Love and self-acceptance does it more easily.

My path was one of pain and suffering. I do not recommend it. I was continually invoking change in my spiritual life, while resisting it with all my strength in everyday life.

Along would come a debilitating bout of suffering, with terrible pain, and as I gradually weakened physically, so my weakness and exhaustion affected body, mind, and emotions. With the advent of collapse . . . came inner change. What a stupid way to spiritually grow.

Unfortunately, it is a common way. Look in any hospital! Whether we accept it or not, life is all about spiritual growth, for we are spiritual Beings.

Pure, simple self-acceptance is so much easier, and pain free. Along with . . . choosing Love!

Beyond the perception of our physical senses,
Truth beckons eternally to the human soul.

Your physical senses give you a wonderful contact with your physical world, but they are unable to take you beyond that. Obviously, the physical cannot take you into the metaphysical.

With the full and constant use of our physical senses a complacency has crept in. People look through *yesterday's* eyes, no longer seeing the new. They look through the eyes of the intellect, seeing *only* what they expect to see.

If we misuse our physical senses so constantly, what chance is there of developing our unknown, and mostly unrealised metaphysical senses?

Beyond the physical range, Truth stands always so gloriously new. If you cannot see the everyday newness of a physical tree, what hope is there of seeing the precious newness of life.

Only through newness can you see and relate to the greater reality in which you live.

JUNE 19th

Consciousness draws to itself physical form through which to express. The expression however, is pure consciousness.

All life is the expression of One consciousness. This consciousness – God/Love – is apparent in all the vast diversity of life on this planet.

Consciousness *is* life. All our natural forms of consciousness are life, including gas, minerals and water, along with all the creatures of Nature.

Always, the *preceding* and *underlying* expression of physical life on Earth is metaphysical, for all consciousness is metaphysical. Realise that the metaphysical precedes the physical.

Most people only become aware of life when it reaches its physical forms of expression.

Our view of life can be deepened by developing that sense of awe and wonder that was inherent in us as a child. A child sees that which an adult – with wonder lost – is unable to see.

You cannot move beyond your subconscious fears
and blocks without the aid of a powerful focus.

Focus is very necessary in all of our efforts in life. Without it we have no real direction. And without direction, we drift aimlessly.

By the very nature of this book, you are likely to be a person looking closely at your life, with the intention of improving it!

Subconscious fears and blocks abound. They are the program of old subconscious conditioning and they strongly resist moving on and moving out. It takes a very powerful focus to penetrate this subconscious agenda. Despite the fact that illusion has no real power, it does have clinging, stubborn habits on its side.

As much as possible, hold a focus on the Truth of your magnificent Self in each and every moment of decisions, in your thoughts, in your words, and in your actions. Where you focus *your* energy flows.

This is how you recreate your life. An excellent focus is to constantly and consciously . . . choose Love!

JUNE 21st

Time helps weave the illusion that humanity calls life.

The movement of a clock: the idea that linear time is an actual, real, true measure of time is exploded when you travel a lot. You cross a dateline, and you have suddenly lost several hours, or a day vanishes as you fly around the world.

Yet we measure life by this fickle, unstable, linear illusion. We believe that when a person is dead, time has run out. We have the false idea that while we are alive we live under the regime of time, and when dead it all comes to a standstill for us.

We need linear time, it gives us cause and effect, but it is not a measure of life – just physicality.

To resist change invokes delay; to delay change invokes reaction; to react to change invokes suffering; to suffer change invokes pain.

Above is the way most people approach change. And I mean Change with a big C. The way that most people attempt change is simply to modify it.

If I have a bronze plate, and I melt it down, to reshape as a small bronze unicorn, people would say it is changed. But no, the bronze is the same bronze – its *shape* modified. It is unchanged.

If I took the bronze plate, and by alchemy, I changed the bronze into gold, the plate would look reasonably unchanged. Yet the change is dramatic; the very substance changed from bronze to gold.

You can change painfully, or you can embrace change and do it gracefully. Change, however, cannot and will not be denied. Modification is not Change! Change is . . . choosing Love!

June 23rd

If you see life through your limits, you experience a limited reality.

Many people will argue from their limits, not realising how little they know. I well remember when once in the UK, a man making statements about life in America. He had never been to America; I had just returned. His so-called knowledge of America came from television! His whole life expressed his limits, but he resisted any efforts to enlarge his view of life.

If you have an opportunity to extend your view of life, or a moment arises when you can move beyond old and comfortable limitations, take it.

Most people have a very limited view of death, completely unaware that death does not end their limitations! Life is endless continuity. To end your limitations . . . consciously choose Love!

Failure to know and experience Truth does not affect Truth. However, it does limit your ability to relate to life as it is, rather than as you see it.

Very few people live and experience Truth. Most people live within the illusions of life, absolutely believing that their experiences and opinions are true ones. They will argue for their beliefs, resisting any statements they could be wrong or deluded.

My Intensives are based on unconditional Love, on emotional healing, and the meaning of life. More than most, I am aware of peoples resistance to releasing old beliefs, old long-held attachments to how the majority viewpoint and beliefs must be right.

This is a huge limitation. Let go of your attachments to how this or that is, or should be. Be open to being wrong. You can never limit the Truth of life, you only limit yourself. Life is vast: we live little crumbs of it.

It helps to . . . choose Love!

*Consciousness can never cease to experience,
to express, or to be. Death is not the denial of
consciousness, only of its physical expression.*

N ot so many people reflect on the miracle and
expression of pure consciousness. I do.

If you take the time to focus on, and connect with
the consciousness of a stone, you find a repository
of vast knowing. And I do mean knowing, as
opposed to knowledge.

In consciousness, knowledge is knowing made
static. Humanity does this, an intellectual trick.
Nature keeps knowing in a flexible state of
constant conscious expression.

What we call the 'unconscious' is no more than a
statement on the limitations of our knowledge of
consciousness.

Nature is the power which creates and regulates life on Earth. Our thoughts and emotions are the power that create and regulate the life we live.

Agribusiness is now moving increasingly into genetic manipulation. This means that farming is moving into opposition with Nature. To oppose the power which creates and regulates life on Earth seems rather stupid. No doubt, it will eventually foster a dramatic confrontation.

Equally, to oppose our thinking process by attempting to not think, or to seek to restrict thought is pointless. Thought is a vast and powerfully creative energy.

All we need to do is take thought and emotion for a walk in the beauty of Nature. Emotions will reveal to thought the full extent of beauty.

It is a beautiful act to . . . choose Love!

June 27th

*Love/Truth is a wave striking the beach. It races
high, smothering the sand in its energy, and the sand
knows the wave. The wave recedes, the sand is dry. It
knows not the wave, nor even its source.*

You are a single grain of sand on the beaches
of humanity. Like an immense wave, Love/
Truth engulfs you in the moment of your birth,
imprinting its essence into your Being.

You then spend the years growing up, usually
growing away from that moment of Love/Truth,
which always accompanies a birth.

You can choose to retain, or reclaim the blueprint
of Love/Truth, or, with the impenetrable shell of
cynicism and doubt established, you can let it all
remain unrealised.

Not a good choice. It is wise to . . . choose Love!

Doubt is a lock on the door of Newness.
Created by the mind in an attempt to maintain
sameness, doubt seeks only the known path.

Our life is a design of ever spiralling into newness. By constantly recycling more-of-the-same, we have lost our way in the swamp of sameness.

History *does* repeat itself . . . endlessly.

I have heard it said that doubt is healthy. If this is so,then why is our world health so chronically poor as self-doubt proliferates and self-worth plummets?

Doubt has no intention of expanding its narrow parameters, nor of opening up. Doubt seeks to maintain limitation; it is comfortable with this.

Introduce newness into your life by consciously being new. Think new thoughts; open the doors to new experiences. Do not allow yourself to be limited by the doubts of friends or family. Live *your* life.

It is new to consciously . . . choose Love!

JUNE 29th

Doubt attempts to destroy trust, but trust is the killer of doubt.

Any situation you are in that holds any doubt at all, simply trust. If you doubt yourself, then look on it as an opportunity to learn to trust.

No matter how much doubt attempts to destroy trust, it cannot win. Trust is the killer of doubt. Trust, and keep on trusting. If it all goes wrong, you can rejuvenate doubt, or you can keep on with the power of trusting!

No matter what it takes, trust, trust, and trust.

In what or whom do you trust? You trust in the magnificent, metaphysical, multidimensional, immortal Being of Love and Light . . . your Self! Never doubt this; you are capable, worthwhile, and powerful. Your power is in your positive action.

Truly, positive action does not get more positive or powerful than when *living* your trust in Self.

Insecurity creates its own insecure reality.

Most people fear financial and emotional insecurity. Of course, they go hand in hand. However, when you think from a place of emotional insecurity, you are the living continuity of your own emotional insecurity.

Whatever it is that you fear becomes your focus in life, and where you focus *your* energy flows. In this way insecurity continually gives birth to more insecurity. All this is based in a focus of *wants* and *have nots.*

Obviously, this does not work for you.

I suggest you create a focus of gratitude and appreciation for all that you *have* in your life. Focus on your blessings. The same principle continues to apply. You are now attracting more and more into your life for you to appreciate.

Choosing Love also assists the whole process.

The thirty-one days of the month of

JULY

Thought for the month:

Most people believe that life is against them, filled with adversity, challenges, and tests. With this belief, life becomes a battlefield, full of suffering and hardship.

Better to realise that life truly Loves you, that life wants nothing more than to support you and nourish you. Let go, surrender to life . . . and trust. Trust in Life/Self/Truth, all One.

JULY 1st

*By your thoughts, by your beliefs, by your
imagination, by your will, you create, guide,
and maintain your life.*

You are the creator of the movie of your life.
Nothing happens by accident or chance, it is all
cause and effect. If cause was sown during a past
frame of your life-movie, when the effect comes
along it is seen as either good or bad luck, chance,
coincidence, or a random accident. Time separates!

Despite appearances, life does not work in this
manner. *You* shape and mould the life you live. *You*
create your fortune and misfortune. It is a good
idea to remember this, and apply it to your ongoing
moment. It is wise to always consciously . . . choose
Love!

The best way to stop thinking is to let it happen!

The more you concentrate on not thinking, the faster your thoughts are racing. Thinking is not really the problem, it is where your thoughts are directed that creates the problems.

Focus on whatever it is that you are doing, give it all your attention, and your thoughts will automatically slow down. Most people do the very opposite. They think about anything and everything that has nothing to do with what they are doing. The result is often mishaps and so-called accidents.

Thought is creative, so be very careful about what you are creating. It is intelligent creation to consciously . . . choose Love!

July 3rd

The language of intelligence is one of accord and agreement: the language of the intellect is one of argument and disparity.

ntelligent argument is an amusing oxymoron. Intelligence does not argue! Argument is the battlefield of the intellect, always looking for the superior statement, often creating debate for the sake of mental stimulation.

Living your life under the aegis of intelligence means that you are not required to argue for, or defend, your beliefs about life, or about anything at all. You can pursue your way of life freely, never needing to explain or excuse. Only the insecure intellect needs to convince others.

*Expressing wholeness, intelligence never wastes
energy. Expressing separation, intellect continually
wastes energy.*

The mind chatters with its intellectual nonsense
all day. By the end of each day most people are
tired or exhausted, yet the energy loss is seldom
caused by the sheer volume of work. Mostly it is
the sheer volume of thought: the weight of anxiety,
of constant worry, and of negative conjecture.

Intelligence is the great conservationist of energy,
expressing itself throughout the day in a way that
conserves energy.

You have as much access to intelligence as any
genius, but you do have to consciously choose it to
use it!

It is rather like consciously . . . choosing Love!

July 5th

If you live your life where you are, now, you
stop falling over your feet.

A lot of people are accident prone, even clumsy, with no physical cause or reason. If you ask them what they were thinking at the time of an accident – and they remember – you will learn usually that their mind was engaged elsewhere.

If you live in the present moment and engage it with your full attention, so many possible and potential accidents will never happen.

It is simple enough to be here, now, but in all honesty, it is not easy. It is however, a practice that I thoroughly recommend. It beats falling over your feet.

Of course, it is also good for your balance to consciously . . . choose Love!

If you can walk along a path of soft grass,
don't go looking for briars and rocks.

Some older people look back on their life and talk about how tough it was. As I look back, my life was tough, but I am very aware that it was I who made it tough.

Whether I could have walked a path of soft grass or not is one of speculation, but I know categorically that I did not have to place as many briars and jagged rocks along the path as I did.

Be kind to yourself. Harshness, criticism and impatience are not good teachers, they create a rough path to tread. Nobody but you decides your life's path, and nobody but you can make it unpleasant.

The best life path is one of . . . choosing Love!

JULY 7th

If you overfeed a racehorse you do not get a Draught horse. Conversely, if you starve a Draught horse, you do not get a racehorse.

Like it or not, we all come into this world with a certain body type. I am not referring to fat or thin that is either an eating disorder, choice, or lack of choosing.

I refer to the structure of your body. You may be strongly built, with a large, hefty frame so you build muscle very easily, perfect for body building. Or you may be slight of build, very slim, the type which is natural for long distance running.

If you are built with the heavy bone frame for muscle and strength, don't think that you can transform yourself into a slim and streamlined, yet strong person. You just get weaker. The same goes for slight and slim wanting to be big, muscular, and strong. Don't even bother.

Be the way you are. You were built exactly right for you. You can certainly develop and maximise your bodily endowments at a fitness centre, but gracefully accept your body type. You will always get the best from your body type by consciously choosing to . . . Love it!

The journey of life is not about more information;
it is about far more participation.

Information has its place in our everyday life,
but so much collected and stored information
stagnates. I have met people who feel safer
because of the huge data of information they have
collected. This is a false security.

Life is about participation. You have to be *in* life,
consciously and with awareness really to be a
participant. Most people are onlookers of life.

Spend one day observing just how much you do
as a consciously aware participant, allowing room
for spontaneity, compared to your customary
subconscious, unaware and regular routine.

Prepare for a shock.

A good way to become a participant of life is to
consciously . . . choose Love!

July 9th

There is no such thing as a clever caterpillar, but they do become beautiful butterflies.

Certainly you can be clever! Cleverness has its place in the scheme of things, but remember, a lot of the time intellectual cleverness holds hands with stupidity. First be conscious and aware, then be clever. This is the *intelligent* way to be clever.

With effort, application, and the use of your inner resources, you can live and express your greatest spiritual potential. This does not require intellectual cleverness.

Be true to yourself, apply the abilities that you were born with, and trust. And always . . . choose Love! In this way you will be able unfold the wings of your greatest potential . . . and fly.

The tree is never in conflict with the wind.

When the winds of life blow, we invariably resist. As soon as we resist, the winds increase and intensify, as opposed to simply blowing.

Mostly we consider the winds of life as bad, as opposing us, somehow depriving us of something. A tree does not live this way. When the winds blow into a tree, the tree offers no resistance; the branches dance to the tune of the wind.

There is no fear in the tree, no idea that it must cling to every twig and leaf. When the wind pulls and twists, the tree lets go of its leaves and limbs. It knows that just as the winds of change work through detachment and removal, so also they bring rebirth and renewal.

Bring this attitude into your life. Realise that these winds also offer you renewal, if you are able to trust life enough to release the old concepts that no longer creatively serve you.

In this unrealised manner, the high winds of life assist you in . . . choosing Love!

July 11th

There is no such state as unconsciousness.

We are told and taught about the collective human unconsciousness; this, however, is illusion.

If a person is hit over the head, and they collapse, this is described as being unconscious. We forget that consciousness is life, and you cannot undo or eliminate consciousness, any more than you can undo or cancel life.

In reality, the person who has collapsed is no longer conscious of being conscious. The hit on the head disconnects the brains connection with physically active consciousness, and the body collapses. There is a profound difference between no longer *experiencing* consciousness, and no longer *being* conscious. This is all rather subtle, but real. Subconscious, yes . . . all too much. Super conscious, yes . . . nowhere near enough. But unconscious, no.

As metaphysical Beings, we are living expressions of consciousness . . . whether we are aware of it, or not!

Knowledge is a floodlight of information.
'Direct knowing' is a spotlight into Truth.

Knowledge is the path of the intellect; it is a valid, well founded and proven path for normal living. The only real problem with knowledge is that it can be stagnant, false, misleading, or inappropriate. Unfortunately, we are usually deeply involved before this is fully realised..

Direct knowing is the path of intelligence. It pertains only to the moment. Unlike knowledge that is encyclopaedic, founded on massive data bases, direct knowing is only involved in what needs to be known in the moment.

Needless to say, direct knowing is a higher, more holistic way of living. In esoteric literature it is referred to as mystical cognition. Basically, it is only available to a person who is holistically conscious and aware.

The same could be said for . . . choosing Love!

July 13th

It takes time to experience timelessness!

Quite a paradox. The experience of timelessness does not just happen – and yet it does. There are so many paradoxes involved here that I am wading through a minefield of them.

As metaphysical Beings we live in a timeless reality, but our physical experience is of linear time. It takes time and practice to let our senses move beyond the confines and restrictions of the physical, to embrace the greater, metaphysical, timeless reality.

I do recommend the effort. While the sceptics and cynics make their judgements of life, you well may experience a reality they have not yet dreamed of.

Timelessness is . . . consciously choosing Love!

To respect life, Nature, and people requires
first a respect for yourself.

You can be born with a respectful attitude, but generally it is something that is learned – and earned. Some people falsely assume that criticism is a path leading toward self-respect, but truly, criticism is a path leading in a very different and opposite direction.

To respect life means that you to have learn to respect yourself. The best way to attain self-respect is to give yourself credit for everything in your life that is good, true, and beautiful.

If by now you see yourself as good, true, and beautiful, then you have already learned to respect yourself.

Treating yourself and those whom you Love with respect, fosters and engenders a respect for life. Self-respect always . . . chooses Love!

JULY 15th

*The heart responds to Love; the mind submits
to Love. Self is Love.*

There are so many techniques published about
how to live life, how to conquer life, how to be
a success in life, how to triumph over life, and so
on, yet truly, all that is needed is for you to find
your own way of expressing unconditional Love for
yourself.

Loving your family – by this I mean *treating* them
Lovingly – is a good way to start. Also Loving your
life – by this I mean a non-critical approach – is a
good way to continue.

When you have unconditional Love flowing in
your life, your heart metaphysically opens like a
flower. The mind becomes submissive, rather than
dominant. And it is all so natural.

A few more reasons to constantly, consciously, and
joyfully . . . choose Love!

Despair is the birthplace of hope.

In the deepest despair, where fear and fatigue tie you in knots of hopelessness, where self-loathing and inner turmoil tear you to pieces, in this terrible place is found the seed of hope. There is a delicate balance between suicidal despair and the birth of hope.

We are each different, each an individual, each with our own story, our own past, our own pain. One person will take the path of suicide, another will hear the whisper of hope.

If you ever reach this place, do not listen to the shout of hopelessness, listen to the small soft whisper of eternal hope.

Hope and hopelessness live together, but they will lead you in very different directions.

You can avoid the empty place of hopelessness by consciously . . . choosing Love!

JULY 17th

Living 'now' is the meeting place of 'being and doing'.

Now ... the world's most exclusive club for humans! Nature lives eternally in the now, we are but rare and fleeting visitors.

Living in the moment while doing our work, or playing, or gardening, or whatever, is where the magical alchemy of 'doing and being' come together ... *being with, while doing to.*

This is the place of miracles. This is the place where we transcend sameness for the joy of newness. This is the place where Nature unfolds its mysteries, where Nature holds its audience with humanity. That is, if anyone is ever in the 'now' ... listening.

Now ... the place of ... choosing Love!

*Anxiety in the subconscious expresses
as worry in our consciousness.*

Imagine a large pond with a deep layer of mud and sediment in the bottom. If you watch such a pond you will notice tiny bubbles continually arising from the mud and bubbling up to the surface.

We will call the pond, consciousness. The mud is our subconscious, where bubbles of anxiety and stress trickle steadily to the surface of the water. As the bubbles ascend ever higher, finally reaching the surface, their energy expresses itself as worry in our subconscious and conscious thoughts.

Therapeutically, working with the bubbles of worry is nowhere nearly as effective as cleaning out the old, sedimentary mud of anxiety.

You can remove the mud by the daily practice of consciously . . . choosing Love!

July 19th

Security contains the roots of fear, while insecurity holds a seed of freedom. The only true security is non-security.

In most cases money is considered the supreme security. My father used to tell me repeatedly, "Security is money, land, or houses." and most people would agree. However, take the money, land, or houses away from a person who has this as their sole basis of security, and you suddenly have a very insecure person.

I do not deny materialism its true and proper place in life, nevertheless, materialism and money, together, hold and hide the roots of fear.

I remember the insecurity I once had. Little did I suspect that seeds of freedom were sprouting in my turmoil, or that I would find the true inner freedom of non-security.

When you know 'who you are', your security is based in your spiritual Self. This is the security of non-security that transcends all so-called material security.

A path to this is to consciously . . . choose Love!

When a person seeks spiritual insight, it is feasible that this may reflect in wealth. If a person seeks wealth, it is unlikely that this will reflect in spiritual insight.

From thirty-five years of age, my main focus in life was my spiritual growth. When I attained spiritual enlightenment, I was forty-nine years of age. This is on a linear scale; enlightenment is non-linear! Be aware also that this was the culmination of many lifetimes of spiritual quest.

Wealth is money in excess of your needs. I do not have this, but I am most certainly a very rich man in the full abundance of life I know men whose life has been wealth based, and yes, they are now wealthy. But that is all. Their spiritual richness is non-existent. And guess which you get to keep forever out of material wealth or spiritual richness!

The greatest investment in the world is to constantly and consciously . . . choose Love!

For as long as you measure your life in terms
of success or failure, you remain unenlightened.

Society labels people as either successful or a
failure. Such labels are meaningless. First, you
cannot measure the success or otherwise in the
life of an immortal Being. What yardstick do you
apply? Money? Fame? Pure foolishness.

No matter how other people may label you,
remember that you are unique. You cannot
compare, measure, or judge uniqueness. Never
try to measure your own life in terms of success
or failure. You can use terms of being happy and
fulfilled, or terms of achievement, these are real,
but success and failure are just ridiculous and
inappropriate terms for an immortal spiritual
Being such as yourself.

Success is the approval of a consensus-reality
society, while failure is its disapproval. We are here
to experience life; experience it in as much of its
holistic fullness and richness as we can.

We can do this by consciously . . . choosing Love!

While soul-Self knows the Truth of our physical reality, identity-self has only a vague concept of our metaphysical one.

During the years of my search for spiritual enlightenment, all the concepts I had of who I am proved to be no more than ashes in the hearth at the actual realisation of Self. Self knows our personal-self so very well: knows and Loves, accepts and approves.

When I see a caterpillar, I often think of how totally unaware it is of the pristine beauty and the ability to fly, just awaiting its moment of biological timing. In a similar way, we are involved in our own metamorphosis.

The big difference is that we have no biological timing awaiting us. We control our own timing. We either activate it, or we do not. But, for all of us, life has a way of painfully pushing things along if we get too slack, or tardy.

To activate your own timing on a daily basis, simply . . . choose Love!

JULY 23rd

*Faith knows not, nor seeks to know, for in
faith this moment is whole.*

We are told that if we have enough faith ...!
even blind faith, just so long as we have
faith.

Have you ever wondered about this? I did. Faith in
God? Faith in life? Faith in what?

The path and key to faith is total trust in Self.

One day I experienced faith, and it was a shock. I
did not suddenly have faith; faith had me. I was
not expressing faith in the way that I had expected,
faith was expressing itself in me.

Let go of all intellectual ideas about faith!

In the fullness and wholeness of the moment an
energy called faith flows through an open and
trusting human Being, and the experience is ...!

Yes, it does involve the daily ... choosing Love!

Time isolates, fear separates, Love connects.

Time and fear have a linear reality, but they are the great weavers of illusion. We are isolated by time, one Earth cycle from another, the child from the aged, the seed from the tree, yet in a greater reality none of this is real.

Fear dominates most peoples lives, caging them in the prisons of belief and anger, separating us from the triumph of One humanity into splintered cultures of dogma and opposition.

Yet there is a way out, a way beyond the snares of time and fear, and that way is Love. Not love as a word, not love as a concept, but Love as a living reality.

We know Love; we all experience it. In times of disaster, Love is always reignited, always with us. Love connects us with life, with each other, with Truth. Love is the universal power of creation.

This is the power of . . . choosing Love!

JULY 25th

Love is a spiritual choice that has never been made if it is not lived and fully expressed.

First, we need to define the meaning of Love in this aphorism. We have the normal human love that is conditional; we also have the more rare unconditional Love. We are all involved in the everyday conditional love, this is human, but the high consciousness of unconditional

Love is what we are here to experience. We all love selectively, but unconditional Love knows no borders or boundaries.

When we Love ourselves unconditionally, we Love all people in the same way. This does not mean there is no discernment in our acceptance of the manner or behaviour of people, but we Love and fully acknowledge that each person is a beautiful soul, no matter how unpleasant or spiteful the personality may be.

Unconditional Love is given birth when, on a daily basis, we consciously . . . choose Love!

Negative thinking kills the negative thinker.
Continuous criticism kills the constant critic.

O f course, there is little to no difference between negative thinking and continuous criticism. Be in no doubt at all that both of these very common practices are long-term serious trouble.

If you are a negative thinker or a continuous critic you are the one in trouble. The subjects of your negative attentions are comparatively unaffected – unless their own thoughts confirm yours – while you slowly but surely bring ever more fear into your life, along with blame and anger, all eroding your family life while destroying your health.

The people who live without indulging in all this unnecessary criticism and negative thinking are generally happy, healthy, positive, and optimistic.

They are the ones who will . . choose Love!

July 27th

*Freedom is not found by changing yourself into
someone you think you should have been.
Freedom is simply 'Falling in love with Self'.*

So many spiritual seekers want to change
themselves into being someone they think is
better. To be better is based in self-judgement, and
there is no freedom to be found in this.

The exultation of inner freedom is found when the
seeking ends; when we accept *who we are, the way
we are,* without any need to judge.

God does not judge us. We do that. We excel in
adverse judgement, self-blame, and self-criticism.
If you are attempting any changes based in one, or
all of these, forget it.

All you have to do is accept who you are, and fall
in Love with yourself. A 'falling in Love' that is both
timeless and endless.

You can achieve this by . . . choosing Love!

The only power and substance to evil is that which people give it.

Where our thoughts and words are focussed, our energy flows. There are religions that spend a lot of thought and words railing against and defining evil, and sadly, they probably think that this is beneficial.

Such a preoccupation is both unnecessary and unhealthy. Evil is not the absence of God, as some believe; an absence of God is impossible. If evil has any reality at all, it is that which we impart to it. We inhabit the same world as the animals and plants of this planet, so how does evil relate to Nature?

It does not, any more than it relates to us. The difference is that Nature simply goes about the business of living in the moment, while we play foolish games of self-judgement and self-blame on the sidelines of life.

It is far wiser to consciously . . . choose Love!

JULY 29th

Linear time gives humanity a chance to grasp
eternity in an acceptable continuous measure.

We are Beings of eternity. Despite this, we think and act like Beings with a very short life span. So often you hear or read quotes, "You are only here once," or "Life is short, so . . ."

What consensus reality rubbish! I repeat, we are Beings of eternity, and so far as linear time is concerned, that is a very long time indeed!

If you think of words like, infinity, endlessness, eternal, forever, you will notice a sort of blank haze creeping through the mind. The mind avoids the very concept of infinity!

Mind and intellect like to work with definable finite concepts, not infinite realities. Sadly, this finite thinking controls and regulates the physical world of humanity, regardless of the fact that we are actually Beings of infinity.

Ah well, next millennium . . . perhaps!

Meanwhile, focus on . . . choosing Love!

Linear time is like ice; the formless, timeless
fluidity of water frozen solid. Let time melt
itself into the flow of Truth.

Although we are physically contained in the prison of linear time, this need not limit us in our spiritual reality. What we spiritually achieve in our life continues with us, to be built on as each new incarnation, or lifetime, unfolds.

I enjoy the story of a local lady who bought for herself a new grandfather clock at the age of ninety-three. She had always wanted one, so when she had the money, she went out and bought it. When the shop assistant asked if she had not left it a little late in life, she told him in no uncertain terms, "I am living and loving my life. Can you do more?"

We have no choice about linear time physically, but in spirit we can, and do, live timelessly.

It is timeless to consciously . . . choose Love!

July 31st

Thinking holds you in linear time; inner silence offers you access to infinity.

The eternal moment is the only place of infinity. You cannot think your way into the moment, so the path is one of silence.

Because we are Beings of infinity, we obviously have access. Certainly it is an access that not many people use, but it is always available. Silence is a portal uncorrupted by time or usage, by neglect or disdain, by contempt or ignorance.

Try it. Try simply sitting in a place that offers you a feeling of being nurtured, and 'listen' to the profound depths of eternal silence.

Expect nothing. Want nothing. And if nothing happens, judge nothing. The secret is in the very rare art of listening.

The thirty-one days of the month of

AUGUST

Thought for the month:

Most people believe that the self reflected in
the mirror is the self they are. This then, is
the basis of criticism and judgement, the place
where illusion rules.

Better to move beyond this 'little' view of life
and realise that Self is endless and boundless.
The self in the mirror simply reflects the image
from the mind, for who sees the true reflection
of Self? The essential Self has no reflection,
other than Love, Truth, and Beauty.

Ironically, these qualities become most evident
when you no longer need to look for them.

August 1st

Spirit is the Intelligence of consciousness.
Soul is the vehicle of consciousness.
Body is the vehicle of soul and the physical
expression of spirit.

People often ask me to clarify spirit and soul, not sure which relates to what. It is also an area of considerable disagreement.

Basically, everything that has body or form is expressing spirit, including a tree, or a rock. Soul carries and expresses consciousness of a more individualistic nature, as in the higher animals, and humanity. Herd animals have a group soul, clearly seen in the synergistic movement of a shoal of fish, or a flock of birds.

In all the forms and expressions of life on Earth, in all the vast diversity of Nature, intelligence is expressing consciousness; consciousness is expressing intelligence.

It is rather like an orchestra and choir joined in a single union of . . . expressing Love!

*Only by entering the overwhelming unknown
can we move from knowledge to 'direct knowing'.
This is a move of epic proportions, a quantum leap.*

The trap here is looking for, or trying to find, a technique that will make this quantum leap possible. Forget techniques. This is not about learning something new, it is about surrendering to a skill that is latent within us all.

The only way you can 'directly know' is by being directly in the moment, and having a true *need* to 'directly know'. Direct knowing is not about gleaning knowledge from a library of facts; it is such a powerful connection with the moment that what is needed to be known is directly manifest into your conscious awareness.

You could say that in consciousness you connect with universal mind. This arises naturally from constantly and consciously . . . choosing Love!

AUGUST 3rd

*Seek not to make the unknown known, for only by
embracing Mystery can we directly know.
Mystery is the metaphysical expression of the
unknown.*

When I write of Mystery I am using the word to
describe the expression of the unknown. I do
not mean mystery as in mystery novels!

For me, Mystery is one of the great excitements
of life. A moment comes when I need to know
something – something that may be defined in an
encyclopaedia, but defined in the way of common
knowledge, and I wish to transcend that. If we live
within our accepted limits, we stay there!

I surrender all desire to know . . . and it happens.
Like a flower unfolding, 'direct knowing' unfolds
into my inner awareness, vibrant, exciting, new.

In perfect timing, Truth and intelligence ignite
a momentous insight into the open, receptive,
conscious mind.

Without death we would become concretised expressions of habit.

D espite our fear of it, death serves us well. Years ago, I heard an aphorism: Death is the creative shattering of habits. Whoever came up with this stated it very well.

As the years go by, most people pick up and adopt ever more habits. A few are dropped off, only to be replaced by others. Habits are rather like concrete, becoming ever more restrictive and set as they age with us.

Elderly people are usually beset with fixed and rigid habits, their life restricted and stressed. As immortal Beings, imagine living thousands of years with the ever growing habit of restriction, limitation, and an ever growing rigidity. We would become unmoving, concretised lumps of habit!

Death is the opportunity to let go of habits and beliefs that are not worthy of us, then we can begin again, refreshed and renewed. Love is never a habit. Life is nourished and enriched by consciously . . . choosing Love!

August 5th

The progress of true human intelligence is always opposed.

In every major field of endeavour, as soon as an intelligent discovery is made that would benefit all people, it is strongly opposed by vested interests of vast wealth, who control, curtail, and manipulate the masses.

Medicine is 'cut and drug' instead of holistic healing; agriculture is 'rape and ruin' instead of working with Nature; inventions are only acclaimed if they maintain the status quo; and teaching is 'cram the intellect' rather than drawing forth our natural intelligence.

Where do you fit into this? Do you live from your true creative, inventive intelligence? Or do you unwittingly follow the path designed to hinder and retard the development and expression of your own unique intelligence?

It is in your interest to always . . . choose Love!

*If you are facing something that frightens
you, the only way through it is to do it.*

When you put off doing something distasteful
it seldom just goes away. The more fearful
the something is, the more negative, the more
likely you are to procrastinate.

The best way is simply to face it, and try your best
for a favourable outcome. More often than not it
goes much easier than expected.

Being frightened of something is generally the
result of negative speculation and conjecture.

You can just as easily project strong and positive
expectations, like . . . choosing Love!

August 7th

Worry is the tortured path, while trust is the high road.

My father was a worrier. A man I knew once told me that he was worried because he knew there was something that he should be worrying about, but he was unsure of what it was! This is the path of sickness and suffering.

When thoughts are left to wander unheeded, they mostly take the habitual path of worry. With great deliberation we need to turn our thoughts toward what there is to appreciate in life. We need to realise that we are both capable and sufficient in our capacity to handle life, and to trust in our ability to do this.

Worry erodes this ability, while trust reinforces and strengthens it.

Trust is reinforced when you . . . choose Love!

When life offers a magic moment, accept the gift.

All too often we find it difficult to accept gifts. Either we feel we do not deserve it, or some other aspect of our past conditioning gets in the way.

The moment of magic, as the world catches its breath and something serendipitous is offered to us, is so often sabotaged.

Unwittingly, unknowingly, in a moment of programmed cynicism, our sceptical-self foolishly thrusts away the unique gift that life is offering.

Let go of these old program's; be open and receptive to the magic of the moment. Give freedom to your wonder and awe, both of which are qualities of the inner child.

You open to wonder and awe when you constantly and consciously . . . choose Love!

AUGUST 9th

Every spiritual inner realisation we have is a deepening of our integration with the holistic consciousness of Self.

Everyone has those moments of inner knowing; those moments when something that we have been groping in the dark for, is suddenly alight with the illumination of an inner realisation.

Mostly we have the everyday types of inner realisation, and we can benefit greatly from this. However, if we are working on a spiritual level that moment of deep inner realisation is not only giving us the insight we were seeking, but on a subtle, more profound level, we are deepening our integration with the consciousness of Self. And as we do this we grow in consciousness.

It helps hugely to consciously . . . choose Love!

Before we become Self-realised we relate to life
life through the mind. When we are Self-realised
we relate to life more directly, while the mind relates
to life through Self.

This change in our relationship with life is truly
a quantum leap in consciousness. Just as mind
tends to project before us whatever it is we are
conditioned to see, believe, or expect; Self projects
that which IS.

The normal persons conditioning will reject that
which IS, unable to face a Truth out of timing.

A spiritually enlightened person, having overcome
the conditioning of ages, accepts that which IS, for
they are now the timing of Truth within Self.

This timing is connected to . . . choosing Love!

August 11th

What we call 'wrong' is usually something we either do not want to happen, do not approve of, or do not understand.

We label so many incidents within life's ever ongoing life-movie of Self as wrong, simply because we relate to life frame-by-frame instead of in a more holistic way, embracing the whole movie. If we do not want it or like it, or simply do not understand it, it is therefore wrong!

You should look at life in a far more open way. If something happens to you that you do not like, examine its circumstances to discover what you can truly learn from the situation. Generally, lessons fully learnt do not have to get continually repeated, so less and less goes 'wrong' in your life – as it is falsely termed.

Life gets much easier when you constantly and consciously . . . choose Love!

Life flows toward needs, not wants.

People mostly speak in terms of 'wants'. The "I want this" or "I want that" litany is a very common one. Self, however, is very seldom impressed by your wants, rather concentrating on your needs. This creates inner conflict. Your identity-self creates ever more wants, while the soul-Self is devoted to your needs.

So, often when you get what you think you need, you don't want it, because you are mostly out of touch with your real needs. In fact, needs can be the very opposite of what you want!

If you are a seeker of Self, release some of those wants, and explore the repetitions in your life to find out what it is that would be to your advantage to learn. When 'wants' and 'needs' come together within you, then life will be smoother and very much more spiritually creative.

It is spiritually creative to . . . choose Love!

August 13th

A spiritually enlightened person views the world
from a foundation of Truth, seeing that which IS.
Most other people view the world from illusion,
seeing that which they 'believe' is.

These two different views of the world cannot be reconciled through argument or discussion. Indeed, to argue for your viewpoint simply indicates your attachment to it, not the truth of it. If a person claiming spiritual enlightenment were to argue for Truth, then he or she has yet to experience it.

The illusionary view of the world is not without value, for it fosters and promotes the opportunity to pierce the illusions of life, thereby promoting inner growth. Never become attached to your own personal viewpoint.

If you say, "This is the way I experience it," you hold the doors open for greater Truth, but if you say, "This is the way it is," then you are holding the doors closed. This takes energy!

It is liberating to consciously . . . choose Love!

While others 'look at', teach yourself to truly 'see'.
While others 'hear', teach yourself to truly 'listen'.

To look at, yet not truly see is the normal daily way of life for many people. When you look at something that is very familiar, you are not truly seeing it the way you would if it were something you had never seen before.

We do not see through the eyes of immediacy.

Equally, we quite easily 'hear' what people are saying, but that is so very different from truly 'listening' to what these people have to say.

We do not listen with the ears of immediacy.

Engage life on a higher level by learning to actually see the newness of what we look at, and to listen to the newness being spoken by the people with whom we communicate.

The newness of life is a precious gift always on offer. Usually it is unwittingly rejected.

Newness consciously . . . chooses Love!

AUGUST 15th

*If you see today's people through yesterday's
eyes, you live as a yesterday's person.*

Few people realise that habit looks through your
eyes, and habit always looks through the eyes
of the past. In this way, the mental and emotional
content of yesterday gets repeated.

If, however, you look at today's people through the
eyes of the moment, open and fresh, then it is you
who live and experience today's new people and
today's new experience.

Newness and sameness sing very different songs.
I recommend that you choose to be a singer of
newness. On my website you can download a
couple of free songs, both take you into newness: 'I
Love You' and 'I Love Me'.

They offer a beautiful way to . . . choose Love!

*Newness is found and experienced only in
the moment. This is indeed, the only place
where Truth and Self may be found.*

How much easier life would be if we all lived,
and were fixed, in the unfolding moment. But,
of course, it would be at the loss of free will!

Living your newness is very powerful, plus you
are involved in the excitement of Self-discovery.
Sometimes when we see an exceptional movie
we may go back to see it a second time, filling in
the blanks and spaces that we did not quite the
comprehend the first time. For most people two or
three times is enough.

When we live in a way that denies the discovery of
newness, and the newness of discovery, we have
to relive and repeat our life-movie over and over,
literally for ages before we finally get the plot! And
the plot is always to live in newness!

Again I say, newness consciously . . . chooses Love!

August 17th

Rigidity offers resistance to life, while
flexibility is ever adaptable to the flow.
Each is a chosen state of mind.

While no one would deliberately choose rigidity, inadvertently we make the rigidity choice if we are not flexible in life. Generally, the more strongly opinionated a person, the more attached they are to their beliefs, they will become ever more rigid.

Rigid and inflexible thoughts and attitude lead to a rigid and inflexible body. As soon as you find that you are arguing angrily about something, let it go. Once you have reached the place of anger you have also reached the zone of rigidity.

Flexibility is a fluid state of mind, while rigid thinking moves us as ponderously through life as an iceberg through the ocean.

Flexibility always . . . chooses Love!

Listen to the collective human song, but
have the courage to sing your own song ,
no matter how different it may be.

We are taught at school to conform. Even where this is resisted, young people still follow the language and fashion of peer groups. There is great pressure to be accepted by our peers, and many a person surrenders his or her uniqueness in endeavouring to fit into a more acceptable common mould.

Be yourself. Express your own uniqueness. Your path in life is your own. The common path is one of consensus reality. Personally, I do not follow this. I am my own person. I encourage you to be true to yourself.

Beliefs that are acceptable by the public do not have to mean your blind conformity. Express your own Truth, be the person whom you were born to be. This is your gift to life.

August 19th

*The fruit of human wisdom will fall gracefully
into your hands when you open yourself to life
in Love and humility.*

Love is – if you like – a strategy of game playing;
the game is Life. Love is a natural expression. It
cannot be forced, nor contrived, and its first focus
needs to be toward yourself.

The key that unlocks the fruits of wisdom truly
is humility. True humility is not the usual false
humility that says, 'I am unworthy.' That is the
cringe of the ego. True humility says, 'I am very
worthwhile, worthy of the best that life can offer
me.'

It takes true humility to see how *Great* you are, not
the false humility of being 'lowly' that crept from
the womb of pious religion. This false humility
is now accepted as the real meaning, probably
accounting for the 'fall from grace' of human
wisdom.

It is your greatness and your wisdom that enables
you to consciously . . . choose Love!

The absence of Truth is the breeding place of misunderstanding.

This seems a very obvious statement, but what is Truth? Is your version of Truth simply a truth you believe in, with perhaps a religious foundation, or is it a universal Truth that is fully supported by all expressions of life?

You have only to look at the endless religious wars to see the conflicts of their little personal truths. Is it a truth that we can fight for peace? Many people believe it!

Where Truth is absent, we get the petty and personal misunderstandings that seem to plague humanity. The way out of this mess is not to be found in the little truths, but by seeking and expressing the greater Truth of Self/Love . . . of 'Who You Are'. Effortlessly, Nature expresses its greater Truth without any intellectual encumbrance.

Surely it is simple enough to . . . choose Love!

Only by leaping into the River of Life do you learn to swim in its flowing energy.

Far too many people sit on the bank of the River of Life, dangling their toes in the water. These are the fearful people, too afraid to commit themselves fully to the variable currents of life that can sweep us away.

These people watch life pass by, unable to come to grips with the fact that life has to be lived fully to be genuinely experienced.

If this is you . . . leap in! You cannot learn to swim in the River of Life by standing safely on the bank. If you leap in, trusting the river, you will find that it supports you fully, whether you are above or below the surface.

However, you learn to dive under the water only after the river teaches you to swim!

You can learn to swim in the River of Life by constantly and consciously . . . choosing Love!

One river in which all life swims: the River of Life. The swim is the Mystery, not the river.

So many people want to understand life, never realising that the river is entirely relative to the swimmer.

Release the quest to understand and define life, because the conclusions you arrive at are no more than fodder for the intellect. Rather, focus on the swim.

The only way to swim in the River of Life is by embracing the Mystery of life. You will swim in direct proportion of your ability to accept this universal Mystery. The more you can embrace the Mystery, the more powerfully attuned to life you become.

Sounds odd doesn't it? Try it, persevere. Mystery and Love hold hands! This is why it is wise to consciously . . . choose Love!

August 23rd

Either you direct the currents in the River
of Life, or the currents will direct you.

It is generally believed that life is something
that just happens, and we react or respond
accordingly. Most people consider that we live
according to the whims of life, or the designs of
God. This is illusion. Life really does not work like
that.

The way you live your life is determined by you. If
you accept that life is an inside-of-Self event, then
you can be the master of your life, finding inner
balance in your choices of daily living. This works
very well if soul-Self and identity-self are in accord.

If you believe that life is something beyond any
ability to direct, being outside-of-Self, then you will
simply live another variation of the familiar theme
of your falsely conditioned past.

Mastery is found by . . . choosing Love!

One river only in which all life swims.
One river, One life. One movement held
in but a single moment. All One.

Oneness is not something that can be easily conceptualised. And even if you can grasp the concept of Oneness, this is still far away from the actual experience.

All life expresses the consciousness of One. Imagine . . . the incredible diversity of One.

Do not try to understand, just get a feeling for the immensity of All . . . life . . . is . . . One. Just . . . feel it. When you are out in Nature, get a feeling for the Oneness of all the life that surrounds you.

Also, when in a city in the crowds of people, imagine – all the consciousness of One. Feel it in your heart. Maybe, just maybe, this may take you beyond the common mental illusion of separation.

To really connect with Oneness, consciously and constantly . . . choose Love!

August 25th

*The direction of your life is very powerfully
shaped by the probability factor.*

I did a great deal of shooting as a young man, so if
I aimed and fired a rifle at a cup on a post, there
is a high probability that the bullet would hit it. It
is very improbable that the bullet would change
its trajectory, expelling its energy in a different
direction.

So it is with our lives. If you have lived with a
powerful focus on perhaps, history, or medicine, or
music in previous frames of the holistic movie of
your life, the probability is that you will pursue, or
be attracted to the same, or similar interests in this
present frame of your life-movie.

This is fully acceptable, unless the attraction is to
continue with a negative outlook on life, or other
unfortunate interests that are contrary to your
wellbeing. If you do not like the direction of your
life, change it.

All you need do is consciously . . . choose Love!

Your birthday is a catalytic time of new probabilities, of new and greater potential.

The energy of birth in each of its annual cycles is quite powerfully catalytic. This is the perfect time to bring to your attention any inner potential that you wish to express, or life-changes that you want to make.

This is the time when new probabilities become most possible. Your birthday concludes a yearly cycle of life, sometimes heralding death – the ending of yet another frame in the ongoing movie of the Continuity of Self. Around eighty-two percent of people die in the couple of months preceding or following their birthday.

Your birthday begins another cycle, when the energy runs with the opportunities of new creation. So use it!

It is the perfect time to begin a new life by consciously and constantly . . . choosing Love!

The intellect is divisive; intelligence is holistic.

Today's Western world worships at the alter of the intellect. Profound intellectual statements are made by scientific organisations, yet many of these statements are not worthy of intelligent consideration.

The intellect looks at life through the eyes of isolation, seeing all life as separate. Intelligence looks at life through the eyes of wholeness, seeing all life as the diversity of One.

Subconscious intellect makes statements about the *web of life,* yet is unable to have even the faintest experience of this sacred connection.

Conscious intelligence experiences the web of life. Intelligence knows that the manner in which you treat any aspect within this Oneness, is how you treat the whole.

Conscious intelligence always . . . chooses Love!

Life is not a journey of the intellect; it is about expressing the unfolding intelligence of Self.

The purpose of schools and universities is to develop intellectual skills. We need this. We also need to have schools that teach the application of intelligence to any problems or situations that might arise in our lives.

As far as I know, the only school to teach this intelligence is the School of Life. And this is a school with a very high level of truancy!

Because we are addicted to thinking – with inner silence a stranger – our thoughts take us out of school. You can only think your way *out* of the moment, never *into* it.

When the School of Life offers us a wonderful insight, or a lesson in humility, we are not ready. We miss it, even when we genuinely desire it. The real intelligence of life's teachings are only in the moment, and we are seldom ever there.

This demonstrates once again the 'being there' of consciously . . . choosing Love!

AUGUST 29th

Anything unresolved in the past, is unresolved now.

All time occupies the same moment. Linear time allows us to play with cause and effect, but this is just one of life's teaching games.

If you have had an issue in one frame of the movie of Self that is unresolved in the so-called past, then that issue is unresolved in the frame we call, now.

If you died grimly a number of life-movie frames ago, or had a really horrific experience, the pain, fear, and misery of that experience will be with you in your consciousness now. It will cast a very powerful influence on the choices you make in your continuing life.

Generally, it is best to face those issues, and go through all the trauma that arises, but this should be done only in timing with your ability to deal with it.

A method that works is the transforming power of Love . . . as in consciously . . . choosing Love!

*You will only know who you are when you
surrender the need to know who you are.*

There are many people on the spiritual search
for Self. Nothing has greater value in the
continuity of your life than to know Self. The
realisation of Self is a quantum leap in human
consciousness.

The paradox is that for as long as you maintain the
search for Self, you maintain the illusion that Self
can be sought.

Surrender all need to know Self, while keeping
your attention on Self. Practice being aware, savour
the moment, relax, and *trust!* It is the intellect that
conducts the Self-searching, yet it will never find
Self, for it is the intellect that creates the illusion of
separation.

A way to know Self is the conscious daily practice
of . . . choosing Love!

To be simple is to be guileless and vulnerable.

A child lives simply. A child is without guile, and accordingly is totally vulnerable. As an adult we cannot be a child, nor do we need to, but we can allow certain qualities of the child within to be expressed through us.

The greatest expression of living without guile is to live without deceit. The deceit that is most dangerous in your life is when you deceive yourself, as in the moments when you say, "I can't," or "I'm not clever enough." All those moments when you deny your abilities, your potential, your Truth, represent the ultimate deceit.

A child has not yet relearned this. A child is very vulnerable to life. Conversely, to be vulnerable is a strength in an adult, for it engenders and promotes trust.

It is a power to consciously . . . choose Love!

The thirty days of the month of

September

Thought for the month:

Most people look into the mirror of life and see the reflection of illusion. They believe in this illusion, adversely judging and criticising it, so gradually eroding the quality of their life.

Better to walk through that mirror, going beyond the illusion into the potential of an expanded reality. This expanded reality is neither fanciful nor conceptual, but it does have to be lived to be actualised, to be brought from its potential into reality.

September 1st

You will never discover who you are through your identity.

Identity dies at the end of each lifetime, at the end of each incarnation, or to be even more accurate, at the end of each frame in the movie of 'The Continuity of soul-Self'.

Practically always, the intellect will conduct its search for Self through identity, not knowing any other way. This means, in effect, that intellect and identity will journey the path of fear together without ever discovering Self – for the discovery of Self is the death of identity.

This does not mean death of the physical body, it means that you no longer relate to life through the illusion of identity. But, intellect and identity do not know this! They can have the stagnant knowledge, but this is not the active *knowing*.

Self-discovery is generated by the daily practice of consciously . . . choosing Love!

Experience is not limited to where your physical body resides.

As a body/identity you are a captive of linear time and a physical reality. As a metaphysical Being, a far wider experience of life is available to you.

Your expression of Self is not limited only to your physical body, thus you can have life expanding experiences while your body is relaxed and calm.

You can 'vacate' the physical body consciously, and while awake, moving into all the dimensions available to your metaphysical Self, for this is your greater reality. This is your cosmic playground! Simply relax, and shift your focus away from your physical-self into, perhaps, a tree, or a flower, or bird, or river, or eventually, even a solar system!

Learn to identify with something in a greater reality, instead of always with your normal physical body. With practice, you may get a very pleasant surprise.

September 3rd

*Intellectually understanding information is
one thing, but to make it real and experience
its worth is a wholly different undertaking.*

L et us say, for example, that as you read the
aphorisms in this book, you understand their
meaning on an intellectual level. Does this give you
their reality? Does this mean you can experience
their deeper meaning fully?

Most people are convinced that to understand
something intellectually on their spiritual path is
all that is required. In truth however, intellectual
understanding falls far short of actual reality.

I made this momentous discovery early in my life,
and I used it with very great benefit on my spiritual
path. Rather than trying to understand as I walked
my path, I simply continued to follow my heart, my
intuition . . . my inner-tutor.

Your heart and your inner-tutor know the wisdom
of my advice to consciously . . . choose Love!

Never take yourself too seriously. But if you are a serious type, let there be 'lightness' in your seriousness.

Having listened while I gave a talk on the Spirit of Nature, a very serious young man asked me if he, too, could see the Spirits of Nature. I then waggled my ears vigorously replying, "Of course, if you can do this."

I tried to keep a straight face as he struggled with many terrible grimaces to waggle his ears, but his attempt was in vain.

"I'm sorry," I said with a shrug, and walked away. He looked devastated. About twenty minutes later, I approached him and asked him why he took me so seriously.

"You're a Master," he replied, "I expect you to tell me the truth."

I laughed. "A teacher has to use any tool that is available, and humour was the tool. Lighten up.

Let playfulness into your daily life. Smile at life. Make room for fun and laughter." It is actually fun to consciously . . . choose Love!

SEPTEMBER 5th

Always live from your strengths, never
from your weaknesses.

It never ceases to amaze me just how many
people live at their most inept level, all the while
criticising themselves . . . and the world. I have yet
to converse with anyone who does not have their
own clear and certain inner strengths.

If you are left-handed this is the way that you
write, use tools, etc. It is no better than right-
handed, simply the way you are. On a physical
level, it really does not matter.

However, your attitudinal approach creates a
very different scene. If you know that you are
a pessimist, then you need be very aware that
pessimism will attract unpleasant situations.

Decide which are your inner and attitudinal
strengths and bring them to the foreground of your
life. Be flexible, positive and open.

Unfailingly, it helps to always . . . choose Love!

People who make negative comments about others simply echo their own unrealised dislike of themselves.

I t is rather like the person who points to someone else to criticise, or mock. One finger points forward, while four fingers point back at the critic.

If I ask a person if they like themselves truly, they generally say that they do, but if I spend some time with them, they usually show me by the content of their conversation, that they do not. And this is not bad or wrong. This is simply the way that most people are.

Listen to your conversation when you talk to other people. If you are critical of others, and continuously making negative comments, you will find that it most likely points to the areas in you that you do not like, including the general direction your life is heading.

To really change your life you need only be aware and conscious. Then, you . . . choose Love!

September 7th

When you see your own 'Light' shining, you
then see the 'Light' shining in others.

When you view yourself through friendly eyes you see a surprisingly pleasing, and beautiful person. The unfriendly reverse is also true!

It is only when you have developed a strong foundation of self-appreciation that you see the true 'Light' of Self at the most unexpected moments of your day. This 'seeing' is really an experience; the experience of being cocooned in 'Light' just when you are in one of your most vulnerable moments.

When these moments unfold their magic, you will see in other people an inner 'Light' that simply shines. This happens only when all judgement has ceased, all criticism ended, and you are seeing life through the eyes of Love.

This happens often when you . . . choose Love!

*Live Now, focussing on the moment, for
herein dwells Truth.*

I write about Truth continually, and quite a number
of people ask me what it is. Truth can be
experienced, but it cannot be described adequately.
The intellect will attempt its own description but, in
reality, intellect will never truly experience Truth. At
best, it is a witness to Truth, an onlooker.

You are a Being of Truth, lost in a game of life that
is at best positive and uplifting, at worst negative
and fearful. And you choose which it will be for
you.

Live with as much focus in the moment as you can.
This is not easy, yet neither is it difficult. When you
are deeply centred in the moment, submerged in
its Mystery, like bubbles of light, Truth will emerge
from Self.

Truth also emerges when you . . . choose Love!

September 9th

To conquer fear, you submit to it.

Whatever you oppose, to that you give energy. Even in a war, the side that is victorious has, all unknowingly, sown the seeds of the next battle. And inevitably, it will happen.

Forget about time, it is not a factor. You are unable to oppose strongly without leaving the anger of that opposition engraved in the consciousness of the enemy. It will germinate and grow. For most people, fear is the enemy.

So it is that people fight their fears; fear of cancer, fear of death, even worse, the fear of so-called failure. By opposing fears, you feed them. Why is this so? Because fear is a self-created illusion, feeding and growing on the negative energy of your own creation.

The way out of this dilemma is to constantly and consciously . . . choose Love!

By allowing yourself to experience Truth you bring about the destruction of fear.

I have said many times, fear is self-created. Fear is based in the subconscious projection of your worst and most painful experiences from your past. Yet in Truth, all this is illusion. The past is illusion; fear is illusion.

If you allow yourself to experience fear, rather than do everything you can to avoid it, you may get quite a surprise. Your fear, when faced, is rather like an old toothless tiger. It appears to be terrible, it sounds terrible, but in reality, its bite is weak and without any real strength.

Only by walking into the very mouth of fear do you discover that it has no teeth. Only by facing its daunting energy do you find that it is no more than an echoing cry from the past, from a place of illusion.

When you withdraw all your energy from fear, there is no fear. By choice, I do not have fear.

The illusion of fear is clearly revealed when, instead of being claimed by fear, you make the conscious choice of . . . claiming Love!

September 11th

Not self denial, nor self hatred, nor abuse
nor ignorance, nor death, nor the illusions
of time, nor even infinity can ever separate
Self from the Love/Light of Supreme Creation.

It is all good news. No matter how badly you live
your life, or how well, you continue to be an
expression of Self. You continue to live within the
spectrum of Truth, no matter how incapable of
experiencing it you may seem to be.

Of course, an acceptance of your Truth offers
you a more holistic experience of life. You are a
magnificent, metaphysical, multidimensional,
immortal Being of Love and Light . . . always!

To accept all this is simple and easy. It is all
revealed and offered if, in daily life, you constantly
and consciously . . . choose Love!

Awakening to Self is the birth of purpose.
Awakening to Self is the purpose of birth.

Enlightenment is the moment of Self-realisation.
It is the moment that you *know* who you are.
It is your holistic purpose in taking on physical
human birth. Spiritual Enlightenment is an aspect
of your reason for Being.

In the moment of enlightenment, a birth takes
place. I could say this birth is the purpose of Self.
I could say it is the purpose of human life, or the
purpose of creation, and all these would be correct.
But if that installed in you an understanding of
your purpose in being human, then I would have
misled you.

The purpose that is born is the substance of
universal spiritual expression; ever changing, so
close, yet so very distant. It is Mystery.

September 13th

You have to cross the 'Gulf of Separation' to realise and 'know' that it does not exist.

The 'Gulf of Separation' is vast and implacable, yet is illusion, without any true reality. I spent fifteen years of my life focussed on crossing that gulf, fully convinced of its all too certain reality. I struggled. I progressed painfully. For me, the Gulf of Separation was a vast chasm to be crossed, and nothing or nobody could have convinced me otherwise.

At a certain moment, the lowest in my life as a person, identity died, and Self stood revealed. In that instant, the Gulf of Separation was crossed, and in the crossing I 'knew' the paradox. The Gulf did not exist. Never had and never will.

It is simple and wise to cross that Gulf of Illusion by consciously . . . choosing Love!

Within the moment there is movement.
Within the movement there is Silence.
Within the Silence there is the ability to 'directly know'.

There are many ways of learning, many ways of gaining knowledge, but in my awareness there is only one way to *directly know.*

Direct knowing can only be experienced in the moment. It cannot be intellectually approached, nor can it be intellectually experienced. *Directly knowing* only happens on a *need-to-know* basis, never on a *want* to know.

Direct knowing only takes place when it is your *timing* to know something beyond all normal explanation. You concentrate on what you need to know, then you release it totally. Eventually, in perfect timing . . . you fully *know.*

It is an all too rare, natural, holistic experience, found only in the Silence of the movement of the eternal moment.

Direct knowing is a result from growing in consciousness. The path is to constantly and consciously . . . choose Love!

Individual action has a universal response.

Many people ask, "What difference can I make in the world? I'm not in a position to change anything." How wrong, they are.

The above question alludes to separation, to the world being too vast and detached for one person to make any difference.

All life is the diversity of One. One human consciousness is expressing the diversity of our personal developing human individuality. What you think and how you act affects the Whole. It is a holistic universe.

Your thoughts, your words, your actions; all are having an affect on life on Earth. The question is: Is your contribution positive and uplifting, or negative and suppressing?

In other words, are you . . . choosing Love!

*Why are Love, Peace, and Acceptance more
difficult to embrace and express than fear,
criticism, anger and aggression?*

C an you think of a reason why it is so for you?
This is simply a question, not an implied or
veiled accusation. Anger was not so much of a
problem for me, but I was aggressive, critical, and
very fearful. And I mean, full of fear!

Now, I am in Love with Self. I accept the worlds
illusions while I focus on Truth, and I experience
profound and deep inner peace.

I say this for one reason; if I can do this, be very
sure that you can also. It is all a matter of what
you choose to dwell on, and express, in the many
thoughts and actions of your daily life.

Inner peace comes from Love. Love comes when
you make the daily choice of . . . choosing Love!

SEPTEMBER 17th

You cannot get out of the cage of illusion while you deny being in it.

When your reality seems the same as everyone else's, and you read about the cage of illusions in a book, or you hear it discussed in a public talk, it is difficult to accept that you, too, might be in such a cage. Generally, there is a moment in your life when the illumination of Truth is presented to you, and you have to make a decision.

I remember when I was in my mid-thirties, and as consensus reality a man as you could possibly be. I was loaned a couple of books on spirituality by a young guy who thought they might interest me.

The books were written by Lobsang Rampa. I devoured those books, but . . . they were so very outrageous! I swayed back and forth. Can I accept this . . . or not?" His words went against all that I knew and believed! But, it really *felt so very right*. I accepted it, and I took a step out of my unrealised cage.

Today, I write the outrageous books that hold the potential to set *you* free! Especially if you consciously . . . choose Love!

Judging and criticising yourself is self-made anxiety and stress.

You would think that criticism from other people is enough, but no, most people are their own worst critics. The idea that self-criticism can in any way improve you is ridiculous. You attract what your thoughts converge on. You attract more to criticise, more to judge, more reasons for the self-destructive energy of stress.

If you were to cease all self-criticism, no longer judging yourself, anxiety would recede and the negative affects of stress would no longer be an issue for you. It is so simple!

Zoom in on your own higher qualities, and direct your thoughts toward the higher qualities in other people.

Remember . . . you attract what you focus on.

Obviously, your focus needs to be on constantly and consciously . . . choosing Love!

September 19th

Miracles are a possibility as soon as you
allow for the possibility of impossibilities.

We are surprisingly quick to declare what is not possible. This is dangerous territory. In fact, we are closing the Door of Life to the miraculous.

Never make declarations of what is possible and impossible. Declare what is possible if you like, but be very cautious about the so-called impossible.

In your own life, what was impossible for you as a child, became possible when an adult.

Surprisingly, some of the things you did as a child would seem to be impossible as an adult. Like sucking your big toe! Yet, with yoga training you might regain the necessary suppleness for this apparent impossibility!

Miracles flirt with the people who are open to the seemingly impossible.

Miracles also appear when you . . . choose Love!

*If you dwell upon your abilities and potential, and
you are relaxed about life . . . miracles happen.*

Some people spend hours daily in a negative
mindset thinking about their shortcomings
and their deficits. This is not a good idea! If you
keep your abilities each day in the forefront of
your mind, registering the potential from feeling
the power of your potential, of your inner vitality,
the pure energy of who you are, then . . . miracles
happen.

You are a miracle. If you have never done so, read a
book about the biological workings of the human
body. Even on that level you are a miracle. Then
consider the fact that you are a creator. You are the
creator of your life. That is truly awe inspiring! Just
think about it.

You create the miracle of your daily life. It is yours
to decide whether your life shall be mediocre or
magnificent, empty or full, hopeless or, dare I
say . . . miraculous.

To create the miraculous . . . choose Love!

SEPTEMBER 21st

All consciousness is One. Individuality is not 'separation-from' the One, it is the experience of 'apartness-within' the One.

Individuality is something humanity is still learning. Read the italics again. And again. In the way of a cloud over the ocean, we are the One consciousness of the cloud, then the uniqueness of each drop of rain that falls on its journey back into the consciousness of One ocean. Cloud, raindrop, ocean . . . all One.

Individuality is the development of each person's unique and special expression of the One. We are inclined to look on eccentricity as an individual characteristic, and, in its way, it is, but mostly it is also an expression of imbalance.

A person who attains spiritual, emotional, and mental balance experiences self as an individual. This is when you know yourself as both part of the Whole, and the Whole in the part. And you consciously . . . choose Love!

Identity is not individuality. Identity is the
expression of separate-self, as perceived
and experienced by the ego.

A child is born, a name is given to the child, and
an identity is established. To be fair, the need
for identity is an aeons-long established habit,
created by the need for identifying each other. Each
time a frame in the holistic movie, 'The Continuity
of Self' comes to an end, both the physical body
and the attachment to identity face death. Each
time there is the opportunity, along with the
body, to allow identity to truly die in death, thus
revealing the Truth of Self.

It is identity that sees the world through the eyes
of separation, for identity perceives self and other
people, self and the world, self and Nature as
separate.

Self experiences all life as One. To weaken the
relentless hold of identity . . . choose Love!

September 23rd

When we create restrictions in our life, we invariably live within them.

We always have a choice. We can live with the parameters of our life clearly defined, accepting our limitations and restrictions as normal, or we can live in a way where we gradually erode their control.

Every time you say, "I can't," you reinforce the parameters of restriction, and you are increasingly confined. With our every thought, and in all our conversation, we are either building more restrictions, or we are removing them.

How about you? Are you reinforcing limits in your daily life, or are you creating new expressions of freedom for yourself?

Freedom is given birth when you constantly and consciously . . . choose Love!

Evil is not a true reality; it is a created reality. The many aspects of ignorance, separation, fear, judgement, blame and anger, create such discord and division in the human consciousness that the resulting mix of expressions are termed as evil when a person embodies them.

For a long time our literature has used the theme of good versus evil as the battlefields of action. With the advent of movies, the theme gained even more momentum, with very graphic detail. Good and evil are deeply imprinted in our collective human consciousness.

For me to tell you that both good and evil, as such, have no true reality is obviously rather challenging. However, this is the reality of Truth.

You need to make a decision about your life: Will you live your life in the old and false beliefs of the past, enjoying the support of your peers, and thus sustaining and maintaining ignorance? or, will you stand almost alone, living a greater Truth that your heart *knows* – but your brain really does not really comprehend? The latter choice takes courage.

This is when you really grasp the benefits of consciously . . . choosing Love!

SEPTEMBER 25th

*All time occupies the same moment. The past
is not past, nor is the future in the future. All life
lives and expresses in the eternal moment. Live in the
moment, and you live in the timeless realm of Truth.*

In Truth, we are spiritual Beings. However, we live
in a physical world, accordingly with linear time
and biological rules.

Unfortunately, instead of living our physical life
according to the nature of physical reality, and
our spiritual life in accordance with our spiritual
reality, we mostly live only a physical life.

Our physical life is short term, but gets all our
attention. Our spiritual life is eternal – and gets
very little attention!

In other words, when we live our spiritual life
according to physical rules, we maintain the
illusions of life, cementing them into a false reality.
We forget – completely – that as spiritual Beings we
are not bound by the physical reality of linear time.

Loosen those physical bonds of illusion with the
daily practice of consciously . . . choosing Love!

When I close my eyes exchanging seeing out for seeing in, I see not only that which is possible, but also that which possibly IS.

A forward vision sees the possibilities of life. Even though it is simple enough to achieve, even this is not common. It was once the measure of a great statesman, but today this ability seems to be sadly lacking in our current crop of world leaders.

An inward vision is far more rare. When the mind is quiet, an inner vision sees beyond the physical possibilities that are held as a potential, to a place where that which IS holds as yet undefined possibilities of creation.

This is something that cannot be taught. A direction can be indicated, but once launched, you are required to find your own way.

The paradox is: If you look for the way, you cannot find it, but when you *know* that you and the way are One . . . it is done.

The way, of course, is by . . . choosing Love!

SEPTEMBER 27th

The only limit to the expression of Self, is self-imposed. However, nothing can limit the reality of Self.

If you were to see yourself with the eyes of true *knowing*, you would see a Being of pure radiance. For the most part we do not see this. If we did, nothing could limit the radiance of our expression of Self.

Unfortunately, our vision is mostly focussed into a purely physical world, feeding us the separation and falsity of its illusions.

The development of inner vision generally requires us to close our eyes to outer vision – but not outer seeing – so that we may see within. Some people take the time to develop this, most do not.

By accepting that you are a Being of Love/Light, and, to the best of your ability living this, to that degree you are expressing the truth of Self.

It all becomes obvious when you constantly and consciously . . . choose Love!

Our lost memory of eternity enables us to pass more easily through the 3-dimensional growth experience we term as life.

Our time on planet Earth is long in linear time. Yet in the endless aeons of the movie, 'The Continuity of Self', it is just a passing flicker in the vastness of eternity.

To varying degrees we all develop a memory of our past, and this memory serves to help or hinder our creation of our future. This is all on the physical level of our self-expression.

On a deeper level it is possible to remember a time before this. It is possible to remember so-called past lives, and even to remember why we chose to incarnate into a physical reality. For some few people, this is a help. For most however, the memories would be a hindrance, an emotional overload that would offer nothing of value on our eternal spiritual journey.

The greatest value to be found on our eternal journey is by consciously . . . choosing Love!

September 29th

Our experiences create our reality, and our reality creates our experiences.

Experience and reality hold hands as we meander through the continuing movie of life. We are not at the mercy of a fickle reality, unless we act in a fickle, thoughtless way. Our reality is our own creation, coming from our accumulation of lifetimes of wise or stupid life choices and experiences.

Be aware of this and avoid situations which rob you of your integrity. Do not put yourself in any situation where you are not being true to yourself. In your daily life, create the reality experiences that most honour you, and keep on creating them.

The more experiences you have that are uplifting, the more you live in an self-sustaining reality. Eventually, people will call you lucky.

You create your own luck by . . . choosing Love!

Life is an ever-expanding mode of infinite realities.

Although we have no choice but to take life one day at a time – and this is enough! – on the level of Self, infinite realities are continually expanding or contracting, according to the deliberate or unwitting choices we make as we live our daily lives. I place strong emphasis on the difference between *aware* and *unaware* choices.

If we limit self, we extend those limits into a far greater reality, eventually experiencing all the repercussions. Happily, the reverse is also true. Creation is BIG, timeless, and endless.

Despite our negative projections into the immediate and greater field-of-realities, in the BIG picture, life has the inbuilt ability to always achieve the most positive creative results. Maybe that is just as well!

To achieve positive, life-expanding results in both the immediate *and* BIG picture . . . choose Love!

The thirty-one days of the month of

OCTOBER

Thought for the month:

Most people believe that anger is natural, that it should be expressed and managed. Some even believe that they find a certain power in their anger.

Better to realise that anger is the unleashed violence of your negativity, and that all anger is unnatural to Beings which are the holistic manifestation of Love. Personal anger is always based in personal attachments.

Better to release the attachment, thereby releasing the anger. Anger cannot remain attached without an attachment!

October 1st

The meaning of life is the meaning of you.

This rates as one of my most commonly asked
questions, "What is the meaning of life?" Well,
now you know. You are! To be more accurate, the
meaning of life is the meaning of Self. So what are
you going to do with this universal knowledge?

You are the purpose and meaning of life. Life is not
an *outside-of-Self* event; life is you, an *inside-of-Self*
experience. *You* are life.

The more meaning you give *to* your life, so there is
more meaning *in* your life.

Consider the import of the word, 'meaning': that
which is in mind and thoughts, to design and
destine, to create purpose. None of this is outside
of you!

You give deep meaning to your life when you
constantly and consciously . . . choose Love!

There is no opposite to God, only opposition.

A great irony of life is that unwittingly, humanity is the opposition to God. By maintaining ignorance and believing in separation, we create and maintain nothing but opposition to the holistic Truth of God.

The belief that God is judgemental is ignorance.

To ignore the Oneness of God is opposition to God. The many religions that use the word of God to condone *their* violence, to advance *their* judgement, and to continue with *their* ensnaring rituals of illusion are all part of the opposition.

Every war, every deliberate lie, all our anger, our negativity, adverse criticism, self-righteousness, Self-denial, on and on, all this constitutes our unrealised opposition to God.

We come into harmony with God/Love when we consciously choose and . . . live Love!

October 3rd

People are locked in the belief that only our
past can effect our future. It is seldom realised that
our future has an equal effect on our past.

Let us look at this in a slightly different way:
All life is created and expressed from the ever
present moment. This is the birthplace, the cradle,
the nursery and the expression of all life on Earth.

In a metaphysical timeless reality, all life is a
simultaneous event, all unfolding and being
expressed as a seamless Whole. Holistic!

The mind can witness this, but for as long as we
use mind from and within a linear reality, intellect
cannot understand.

The ripples of effect radiate in all directions, just
as easily sweeping from the future to the past, as
from the past to the future. The central point of all
movement is in the immediate moment.

Our everyday linear viewpoint of life is based in
separation and it's subsequent illusions.

You can fracture these illusions by consciously
living and choosing . . . unconditional Love!

Life rewards the lovers of life, for they act from true innocence.

I was not always a lover of life! This is something that I had to learn. But as I slowly learned to Love myself, so my relationship with life changed; I fell in Love with life. A child begins its life with a deep sense of trust. They trust their parents, yet all too often the parents are untrustworthy. This makes no difference to the naivety or innocence of a child.

When, as an adult, this rare and childlike approach to life can be maintained, then a Love of life is born that will endure, enriching the persons life.

Carolyn and I both Love our lives. We consider that we are very blessed in our relationship with each other, and life. Right-brain and naive, we are two of life's natural innocent lovers. This innocence can only be given birth after a long and sufficient gestation, nurtured in the heart of a loving relationships with self.

It is ably assisted by consciously . . . choosing Love!

OCTOBER 5th

The profound and universal question, 'Who am I?'
cannot be asked with any true meaning until
the experience of the answer is within your
aware consciousness.

The 'Who am I?' question is asked by very many
people. However, for as long as it is the intellect
that asks the question, the question is empty of
meaning, the answer unobtainable.

When the 'Who am I?' question arises from the
very depths of your consciousness, exploding
unexpectedly into your conscious awareness with
the shattering impact of a bomb, then the question
and the answer are One, absolutely inseparable.
Not that you will have the slightest awareness of
the answer experience!

When the question shatters your whole life, and
you are driven to know Self, driven even through
your own self-derision, your unwanted resistance,
your own humiliation at the shreds of your life;
it is only then that you will know the impeccable
timing in the inherent power of consciousness.

To bow before a humble tree takes but a moment of your time, while that which you may receive fills all the spaces of eternity.

What can I say? Try it. Release all your thoughts, let the mind be still, feel the vastness of life within the tree - it is All life you feel - and bow in humble awe to the mystery that is a tree.

You need to abandon the concept that humanity is supreme on planet Earth, realising that All Life is One. Life is a mystery you have yet to comprehend, but Nature can teach you of Truths undreamt.

A Truth undreamt is the moment of realisation that eventuates from constantly and consciously . . . choosing Love!

OCTOBER 7th

Oneness is not the sum total of all its scattered parts.
Oneness has never been fragmented, separated, or
divided. All life is One.

When all the explanations of Oneness are spoken, written, and finished, Oneness remains as no more than a concept to the baffled intellect. The intellect creates separation in its isolated view of life, so its explanations of Oneness are futile.

Oneness is the experience of the connectedness of all life. In any moment, birthing, dying, or any instant between, you may experience Oneness.

You cannot order it, you cannot manipulate it, you cannot force it, nor can you meditate for it. All you can do is to allow all want, all desire, all attempts to understand Oneness to expire . . . in perfect timing!

The greatest path to Oneness is found by the proven formula of consciously . . . choosing Love!

Nature does not need to be saved; Nature needs to be honoured. The problem is you cannot honour Nature if you do not honour Self.

Many very caring people want to save Nature. While I think that these dedicated people are a wonderful example to us all, only a few of them seem to comprehend the bigger picture.

Human devotion to saving a species is a wonderful energy to inject into consciousness, but as well as saving a species, Nature as a whole needs to be honoured.

By honouring Self, you honour all life. It may appear very noble to devote a life to saving a species – and it is – but not if the people concerned lose sight of the greater picture of all life as One.

Nature is the power that creates and regulates the world. If you accept Oneness to mean that all consciousness is One, then nothing in Nature is in jeopardy. If you believe in separation, then there are species that are in danger of extinction!

No matter how deeply we get caught-up in the illusion of separation, the way out is to constantly and consciously . . . choose Love!

OCTOBER 9th

Patience and attitude precipitate the flow.

The flow is the movement of life's abundance. For many, life's abundance is a concept, words that encourage, may even inspire, but have no real meaning for them. Such people are often impatient with life, struggling for the benefits that life seems to deny them.

Develop an attitude of gratitude for what you already have in life. Learn to be patient with yourself, for it is not life that has to learn anything, it is you. Patience combined with appreciation is active; patience as in simply waiting is passive. If you wait for life, life will wait for you, and not much happens. If you wait with aware gratitude, then by your participation you activate the flow.

Need I say that the flow is also activated every time you consciously . . . choose Love!

Understanding is usually inappropriate for our spiritual journey. Mystery is Truth unrealised. Most understanding is based on a conceptual rationale, rather than actual realisation.

Understanding is a valid challenge for our everyday life in a world of ever-increasing technology. On your spiritual journey – which is the soul purpose of you being here in the first place – understanding is an anchor that will snag on every intellectual obstacle in your immediate vicinity.

The way to make your spiritual journey as smooth and trouble free as possible is to eschew all need to spiritually understand it.

Accept the Mystery. Accept that while Truth is unrealised, understanding is useless flotsam on a vast ocean. It will not support you!

When you reach the shores of Truth, you will *know* just how futile that intellectual flotsam was!

Even though you may experience it, it is unlikely that you will ever truly understand the power of consciously . . . choosing Love!

October 11th

When wisdom whispers its Truth in your heart,
accept it. To empower this Truth, live it. In this way
you become illumined by Truth.

People are mostly too caught up in the hurry
and scurry of life to listen to their inner voice.
Moreover, the mind is either shouting its negative
nonsense, or chattering to itself like a demented
monkey.

Generally, cleverness resides in the brain, while
wisdom resides in the heart. The brain shouts,
demanding your attention, yet the heart whispers
softly, waiting for you to register and acknowledge
its presence.

In our society today, the heart is so very neglected.
It is not by chance that heart disease and sickness
is so prevalent. If you are not in harmony with your
heart, then you are not in harmony with your body.

Listen to the whisper of your heart, and have the
courage to live what you learn. The quiet whisper
of wisdom will constantly recommend that you
consciously . . . choose Love!

I close my eyes and, in the closing, stars wink out.
I dream of a long forgotten past, of a future I once
knew, and in some other reality, I experience déjà vu.

Maybe this inspires some spark within you. It concerns the wonder, mystery and vastness of a multiverse.

I will not pursue it here, yet I must state that we live in a multiverse, not a universe. Our universe is one of a multitude.

If you release your identity-self, moving into the consciousness of the metaphysical Being that you are, the future and the past become basically irrelevant.

If you can learn to release identity, expectations, thoughts and desires, in essence, you can be *anywhere* or *any-when* metaphysically.

October 13th

Truth is always Truth, yet only in a person's timing to embrace Truth, is it Truth for them.

Truth is always Truth, yet out of timing it is not Truth. In other words, if, on reading some of the aphorisms in this book, you find Truth resonating in your heart, you may feel inspired to share it with a close friend.

Don't be too surprised or disappointed by their negative reaction. They might tell you that the aphorisms just don't make any sense.

For them, they are right. For you, you are right. A higher Truth is only Truth in timing.

Have the courage to follow your own truth, even if you appear to stand alone. It is a higher Truth with its own timing for you to constantly and consciously . . . choose Love!

*The way that you live your everyday life is the
expression of your thoughts, attitude, desires,
emotions, ambitions, etcetera.*

In other words, a person who thinks thoughts of
anger is an angry person. A person who has loving
thoughts is a loving, caring person.

How about you? Hugely common are worry
thoughts. Most people are continually worried.

Anxious thoughts, guilty thoughts, negative
thoughts, blame thoughts – these are the thoughts
that create the reality of the non-aware thinker.

Aggression creates an angry attitude, while
fearful expectations create a person lacking inner
fortitude. Continual feelings of despair generate an
emotional energy of depression.

Accordingly, choose your thoughts and feelings
with care. If you think you cannot choose, you have
just chosen apathy!

Obviously, this is my cue to remind you to
constantly and consciously . . . choose Love!

October 15th

The more we seek to avoid something we fear, some-thing unpleasant, the more strongly we attract it. We magnetise emotionally that which we most fear.

When fear becomes a major preoccupation, it is always emotionalised. Despite fear being an illusion without any true substance, we give it the substance of an emotion saturated with its negative load of worry and anxiety.

If there is something you fear in your life, then confront it. Face the fear and deal with it. Just about always you will find that by facing it squarely the fear was easily conquered.

A fear faced is a fear released. A fear that is grimly held by your negative emotions becomes a very heavy load. The longer you carry this load, the more it will attract the circumstances and situations that you most fear. Be aware also that fear, hopelessness and sickness walk hand in hand.

To erase your fears, consciously . . . choose Love!

*What identity-self calls an accident, soul-Self knows
as unrealised purpose.*

When we see an accident on the highway, or
we are involved in one, there is a period of
shock, sometimes with deep grieving.

It is called an accident, even though we look often
for someone to blame, perhaps to be sued. This
is not wrong, but it is part of the illusions of life.
Blaming and suing simply perpetuate the illusion
of separation.

In the reality of Oneness, there can be no such
thing as an accident. What we call an accident is
an expression of hidden, unrealised purpose.

Anyone with whom you are involved in a so-
called accident, are people with whom you have
interacted in past frames of your life-movie, and
most probably it was a negative interaction!

Instead of blaming and suing, look for a final
resolution for all involved. If this is rejected, you
can always find resolution for yourself by acting
from . . . unconditional Love!

OCTOBER 17th

Righting wrongs judges and separates,
acknowledging wholeness uplifts and connects.

We still have crusaders looking for wrongs to right, or causes for which to fight. People with a knightly hangover!

To look for what is 'wrong', you have to make a judgement. How can you judge when you do not know the life-movie of that person? Life reveals the law of cause and effect over the period of your whole life-movie, rather than in just a single frame, a single lifetime.

As we go through life, we are required to make many evaluations of people, determining their faults and merits. If we do this from a holistic viewpoint, we find that our evaluation is based on discernment, rather than judgement.

We develop our ability to discern every time we consciously . . . choose Love!

Nature's evolution is a response to environmental changes, coupled with the pressure to survive biologically. Nature's pressures are external.

The tree that sheds its leaves each autumn is following a pattern of survival. As precarious as hibernation is for all the creatures that are involved, it is all about biological survival.

There was a time on this planet before the ability to hibernate when creatures simply died in the extremes of cold. So Nature came up with a survival program, and made the necessary evolutionary changes.

All Nature's evolutionary pressures come from the environment, ranging from changing weather patterns to deep oceanic currents and planetary changes, and Nature adapts to them.

All this takes place on both physical and metaphysical levels, an expression of Wholeness. There is no resistance to any of these changes because Nature is all about growth via change.

October 19th

Human development comes from a response to mental and emotional pressures, coupled to the soul. Human pressures are internal.

Human *reaction* to internal pressure is why we get locked into the 'more of the same' syndrome.

As technology advances, our thinking needs to change, yet we continually resist change. It is our fearful resistance to change that causes our emotional conflicts to remain unaltered.

Fear reacts, avoiding inner change.

If we were to *respond* appropriately to those pressures we would grow into a new order of human expression. Lifestyle and technology are all external to us, and so easily embraced. It is the inner changes that we strongly resist.

Love responds, embracing inner change.

This is just one of the many reasons why I do my very best to convince you to constantly and consciously . . . choose Love!

Insecurity create its own insecure reality.

Mostly unrealised, it is our thoughts and emotions that create our reality. It becomes obvious that if our thoughts and emotions are insecure, then we have no choice but to maintain the very reality that is causing us so much distress. Clearly, this does not work in our favour.

The art of living is to create the thoughts and emotions that are the very opposite of insecurity feelings. In other words, when you are feeling insecure and threatened, you need to consciously appreciate all that is in your life, knowing that despite appearances, you are lovingly supported, and that all is well in the divine plan of your holistic Being.

Not easy, true, but it will change your reality from being insecure to one which, although probably not yet secure, is at least heading in a far more positive and uplifting direction.

Add to this a sustained effort to create change by consciously . . . choosing Love!

OCTOBER 21st

A linear time structure maintains our belief in past and future, beginnings and endings. Spherical time is based in an holistic reality, indicating that all time occupies the same moment.

Conventional thinking might conclude that a war won is a war finished. Wrong. The lesson of history suggests that a war won is just the beginning of the next stage of conflict, however long that may take to come about.

We live in a time structure that has biological beginnings and endings, and we instinctively extend that beginning and ending theme into our entire lives.

We overlook the fact that as spiritual Beings our life has no beginnings, no endings. We truly are Beings of eternity. 'Sow and reap' expresses itself over an almost endless time frame. There may well be long pauses between sowing fear and reaping pain, but like an appointment with the dentist, it inevitably arrives.

Sowing Love is the only way to go. When you reap the harvest of Love you will smile indeed. Maybe this is why I encourage you endlessly to constantly and consciously . . . choose Love!

With the birth of individuality, the concept of separation came crawling from the same bloody womb.

In the shaping of humanity, we were given the opportunity to experience individuality. However, we were required to make a choice, for choice is absolutely essential in the birth of individuality. Without choice, individuality cannot be born.

Instead of choosing to be an individual *connected to* the Whole, inadvertently we chose to be an identity *separate from* the Whole. Not a good idea!

Although this choice could never change the reality of what IS, it does mean that instead of evolving and growing with Oneness, we are doing our best to evolve and grow under the deceitful influence of the illusion of separation.

To return to the positive and creative influence of Oneness, all you need do is . . . choose Love!

October 23rd

Fear was the midwife at the conceptual birth of separation. The attendants were desire, greed, suffering, and anger.

Note that I state 'conceptual birth'. In Truth, neither fear nor separation have any reality, so the birth of separation is but a concept.

Unfortunately, it is a concept that is so strongly imprinted in human consciousness, in the very structure of our society, that many people dare not change their beliefs, or their view of life.

This has unpleasant repercussions. While you maintain the illusion of fear, you also have to live with all the many expressions of negativity and suffering that accompany it.

The way out of this is as easy and natural as releasing your subconscious fears by constantly and consciously . . . choosing Love!

The more fixed and rigid our belief system, the more vigorously life will shake us to detach our fearful grip.

Similarly, the more flexible and open you are, the more gentle will be life in revealing your inner Truth to the enquiring mind.

My late wife, Treenie, had a favourite expression that she used frequently, "Let go, let go, let go."

If you were easily able to let go anger, frustration, fear, blame, desires, guilt – it's a long list – you would not be so savagely shaken by life in the way that most people are now experiencing.

I never met anyone who actually wanted to hold on to any of these negatives, yet I meet so few people who can easily detach themselves from them. If you have a 'holding on' habit . . . 'let go'!

Love never attaches. So another way of letting go is to constantly and consciously . . . choose Love!

October 25th

*The parameters you lived in yesterday will be the
same parameters you live in tomorrow, unless you
change them today.*

Nothing in your life will change of its own
volition. The way you lived yesterday is going
to continue until you make the required changes
for inner growth and expansion in your life.

It is unfortunate that so many of those borders and
boundaries in our life were set and fixed when we
were children, often by observation of our parents.
Much as you may have loved your parents, you do
not want to live within the same parameters that
they did.

Beginning today, look at the boundaries that
delineate your life. Accept that you do have them,
and then decide if this is the way you want to live
for the rest of your life.

We are rather like potted plants. If you want the
plant to reach its full size and potential, you have
to keep on transplanting it into bigger pots.

We definitely stretch our boundaries if, on a daily
basis, we consciously . . . choose Love!

Where there is inner peace, there is no criticism,
judgement, or anger.

Even when you live with inner peace, the world
continues with its challenges and opportunities.

Sometimes it is a challenge not to be frustrated
when delayed at an airport for eight hours, but as
soon as you focus into your centre – that place of
inner balance – peace is paramount, the delayed
hours just a passing inconvenience.

My lovely wife Carolyn often says, "There is
nothing that is worth giving away your peace."
When these moments happen to me – and they do
– I say to myself, "This too will pass." And it does!
There are more than enough people who are angry,
critical, and judgemental, and sadly, far too few
connected to their inner peace.

Finding your own inner peace – and living it – is a
great personal contribution toward world peace.

Peace is easily found when . . . choosing Love!

October 27th

For every year that passes, either the subconscious or the conscious mind grows more dominant in your life. To allow the subconscious mind dominance, do nothing. For the conscious mind to become stronger, you will need to focus on, and practice, awareness.

Most people are incredibly unaware of the moment, of Self, of creating our own reality. And many people do not want to know about it. They react with scepticism and derision to words such as these.

As I have said, life is about choice, and having to live our choices. I strongly recommend that you regard yourself as a deserving, wonderful person. Listen to your thoughts, your casual conversation, and become aware that this is the life you are creating and living.

When you live with a greater awareness of your daily life, you will be happily surprised by the extent to which life is continually attempting to reveal a greater reality to you.

Your reality is greatly enriched when you continue to consciously . . . choose Love!

Unenlightened action produces unenlightened results.

An action from a spiritually unenlightened person produces results that are more likely to reinforce their illusions of life, than to enlighten them.

However, actions that have a steady regard for spiritual wisdom, and have an openness to a more holistic life will attract those spiritual insights that inspire the flowering of the soul.

Acting with an awareness of Self, with a respect and acceptance of self and other people, will lead you toward more enlightened results.

It is an enlightening choice and action to constantly and consciously . . . choose Love!

October 29th

Those who want to believe the worst and most negative will do so, while those who choose to believe in the best and the most positive will do so. Seldom, however, do you find these people in the same company.

Without any judgement of these two types of people, with which set do you mix?

If you mix with the more negatively inclined, this is where you are at. You should recognise and register this fact. If they are more positive people, then this also reflects in you.

The people who linger on the edge of both expressions certainly mingle together, though those who live the extremes do not.

Make a clear choice about what you want in life, and socialise with the people who express and support the values you consider important.

The friends to mix with are those very few wise people who consciously . . . choose Love!

The great purpose of life on Earth is to combine with, and through our living, express the creative uplifting power of unconditional Love.

Unconditional Love is alive on this planet, but it is rare. Most normal love is expressed through conditions, probably the most common being the unspoken: I love you if you love me.

There are no conditions to Love. Seriously, if you place conditions on your love, then you are not expressing Love; you are expressing the conditions for your emotional favours.

I have heard it said that we do the best we can. Do we? Do you? I had to learn the true meaning of Love long after I thought that I was *in* love.

If you are doing the best you can, each day you are learning more and more about how truly and selflessly to express your unconditional Love.

If, day by day, you are not learning this, then you are most certainly not doing the best you can.

Day by day, consciously . . . choose Love!

OCTOBER 31st

The inner words of Silence are not meant for the intellect, with its erroneous interpretations and rationalisation. They are meant for the ever open and hungry soul.

So much food for the intellect in our busy world of Internet and technology, so little food for the spiritually hungry soul.

Do you take the time to nourish your soul-Self?

Do you consider the spiritual needs of the soul you are as equal to your physical needs?

Do you spend time in quiet contemplation of the spiritual aspects of life?

Do you take the time to meditate?

Do you sit with Nature?

Work, enjoy yourself, have fun, be happy, do what you have to do, but remember, if you leave your soul needs out of the equation of life, you are going to experience a lack of soul fulfilment, and the inner hunger will grow.

It is food and nourishment for the soul when you constantly and consciously . . . choose Love!

The thirty days of the month of

NOVEMBER

Thought for the month:

Many people consider that taking risks is both unnecessary and undesirable. They fear making an error, fear the consequences, choosing safety and security rather than the possibilities of risk.

Better to realise that safety holds hands with stagnation, and that while risk is a threat you continue to maintain the fear/threat of risk.

The fear of risk is based in the possibility of short term loss. You are an immortal Being, so . . . what is the risk?

NOVEMBER 1st

Complicated thinking weakens purpose, while simple thoughts are empowering.

Every time I hold my 5-Day Intensives or give public talks, I continue to be surprised by the complicated thinking of so many people. It is as though people strive to look at life in the most convoluted and tortuous way that is possible. Thinking in this way weakens your resolve.

So often a person seeking my advice has progressed into an ever more complicated tangle of muddled thoughts and words.

"Do you fully understand your question?" I ask.

"I think so," is a usual reply. Such is confused thinking, forever clouding the issue.

Quite often, when you can state a question simply and with absolute clarity, you will find your own obvious answer.

More often than not, the simple answer is to avoid confusion by consciously . . . choosing Love!

Beyond the DNA, yet expressing itself through the DNA, is the Song of Life – the quintessential translation of pure, Divine Intelligence. Self is One with this Divine Intelligence.

Science is the systematic study of the nature and behaviour of the material and physical universe. Fundamentally, science ignores that which is beyond physical reality, the area of metaphysics and meta-science.

However, apparently science is now studying pure intelligence, as well as looking for the evidence and expression of intelligence in Nature. It would seem to me that this must surely eventuate in science reluctantly meeting with metaphysics. I would like to be there!

Pure Intelligence expresses through 'all' life, meaning: the animal, vegetable, mineral, even gaseous, as well as metaphysical and ethereal kingdoms.

Pure intelligence consciously . . . chooses Love!

November 3rd

You are unable to express free will while you are held in the boxes of your beliefs.

I f you are raised by Buddhist parents, you grow up with a Buddhist view of life. If you grow up in a Catholic family, you have a Catholic view of life. The same with Hindu, Muslim, atheist . . . or whatever. The formative years of your life were spent subjected to a particular set of influences, which literally boxed you in.

Obviously, you cannot be in a box and be free. While you hold strongly to any beliefs, you are attached, and attachment is not freedom!

It takes courage to step out of a box that may well contain your whole family, but if you are on your spiritual path truly, you have no choice.

As soon as you dogmatically resist, you are in another box. It is the same old story . . . surrender it all, release it all.

Except, of course, consciously . . . choosing Love!

Abundance is not found by focussing on what you want; abundance is found by appreciating what you already have.

Many people are almost totally preoccupied with thinking about the thousands of dollars that they would like to have. To this end these people enter lotteries to win money, a house, a boat, car, motor-home, anything!

Even if you win, abundance does not manifest itself this way. At best it is short term gain. Real abundance is a state of consciousness.

You find this inner state by appreciating fully the 'hundreds' of dollars that you now have.

When this 'feeling' of appreciation is deeply established, then you will find that 'thousands' of dollars are being attracted into your life.

Too simple? Try it! Where you focus, energy flows. It is the same as the Love principle: to constantly and consciously . . . choose Love!

November 5th

Generally, each person is his or her own greatest challenge. Put simply, this means unconditional self/Self acceptance.

There are two layers to this. The most basic layer is to accept yourself for the everyday person that you are, warts and all.

This level of self-acceptance implies that on looking in the mirror, you feel acceptance for your body, your features, for all of you. It also means no self-criticism!

The next layer is the acceptance of Self.

No point in looking for Self in the mirror. This layer is only found when the necessary level of self-acceptance has been achieved.

Be gentle with yourself. Be appreciative for all that you are. Too many people focus on what they could be, with resultant discontent. And discontent always generates yet more discontentment.

You grow and develop self/Self acceptance by consciously . . . choosing Love!

We already 'are' that which we are becoming. This means, in effect, that we must replace 'becoming' with 'being'.

In the statement 'I am becoming wiser', is the built-in implication that 'becoming' may continue for a very long time.

However, if you state, 'I am wise,' you are now claiming this inner state. And 'now' is the operative word.

Most people are afraid to make this sort of claim, fearing that it is arrogant. It has nothing to do with arrogance: it has everything to do with self-assertion. In fact, it is wise to claim your wisdom.

'Being wise' is much wiser than 'becoming wise'! It is daily wisdom if you constantly and consciously . . . choose Love!

November 7th

The prison that contains you is made of the limits you place on being free.

During conversations at an Intensive, I sometimes ask a discontented person why they are not free to be the person that they want to be. By this, I do not mean the so-called freedom of a democratic nation, but the personal freedom to express yourself fully in an holistic way.

Generally, in reply, I get an account of how the person has to meet their responsibility as a spouse, partner, parent, pay off the mortgage, create a reasonable income, all this, along with a few other problems that frequently arise with modern living.

I then reply on the lines of the foregoing aphorism.

It is possible to meet all the responsibilities of your life ... and be free. But you do have to consciously choose freedom – and live it.

It truly is as simple as creating a daily focus on consciously ... choosing Love!

It is your own adverse judgement and criticism of yourself that, by isolating you from your greater Truth, denies you your birthright of inner peace and inner freedom.

I guess I have said this many times in these pages, but really . . . quit all judgement and quit all self-criticism. Trade-in criticism, and,in its place, use self-appreciation. Release judgement, and try gratitude instead.

Your life will be so much happier, so much easier, you will wonder what happened.

Your birthright is always with you, always waiting for you to claim it because you already own it.
If this seems to simple to be possible, always remember . . . simple is powerful.

This is a gift only you can give to yourself, along with the gift of . . . choosing Love!

NOVEMBER 9th

When fear dominates your life, separating you from Truth, fear makes all the choices. Fear never chooses honour, or Love, or any expression that is not based in fear.

This describes the life of so many people. Is this your life? Do you make all your choices free of fear, or does a deep, hidden, subconscious fear continue to make them?

I can remember, many years ago, when I milked about a hundred cows. It took me eight weeks to learn that I really did not like milking cows. I liked cows, but not the twice a day, two hour procedure of milking them.

When I sought the reason why I was milking cows, I had a shock. I realised that fear cracked the whip, and acting from the stimulus of fear, I bent my back – cowed!

Eventually, after eight years of inner growth, I chose to honour myself. That, in turn, took me away from milking and farming, leading me toward a whole new way of life.

A way of consciously . . . choosing Love!

In all its many different expressions, self-denial versus Self-acceptance is one of the major conflicts of life and living.

Every time you say, "I can't," you reduce yourself. Even thinking it, diminishes you. Every quiet criticism of yourself, in whatever way, is a denial of your Truth.

Truth . . . you are a magnificent, metaphysical, multidimensional, immortal Being of Love and Light. Can you accept this, thus empowering Self? Or do you think it highly unlikely that you are a Being of Love and Light?

It is so easy to deny soul-Self by denying your identity-self. Why is it so difficult to accept that you are a magnificent Being? It is Truth.

Assume the mantle of your power by living the joyous affirmation of your Truth.

You affirm it every time you . . . choose Love!

NOVEMBER 11th

Why is it that human cultures invariably spotlight their few basic differences, rather than their many fundamental similarities?

Why is that people look for what is wrong in themselves, rather than for what is right?

I have no doubt that if people were to dwell on everything on which they approve in themselves, they would see these finer qualities in all people, regardless of cultures.

We are One humanity. Although cultural diversity is very apparent, and even human expressions, we still laugh and cry in the same language, we still experience pain and hunger in the same way, we bleed the same colour blood, and we all feel the same inner hurt from hostility and intolerance.

It all begins in your relationship with yourself.

Surely the answer for all peoples and cultures is to always consciously . . . choose Love!

That which uplifts and elevates humanity does the same for Nature and planet Earth. We are One. Equally, those actions that plunder and defile Nature and Earth, are detrimental to all humanity.

Once upon a time, agriculture had a noble methodology and intent, based in simply feeding people for a fair financial return.

Now, most of our agriculture has so changed in its purpose and expression, it has become agribusiness. True culture of the soil has been abandoned, except in organic farming. Instead, the land is destabilised and exploited.

Agribusiness is the exploitation of the land for profit. The cost is defiling Nature.

No matter how unbelieving we are, or how we ignore a greater reality, *the cause* that we sow into our planet Earth will create the harvest *we reap* Indeed, this is a harvest that all of us will reap.

I am serious when I say that the impact of this unwelcome harvest may be personally reduced if you daily and consciously . . . choose Love!

NOVEMBER 13th

We each create our own reality. By living the reality we create, and by recognising that this is our creation, we can get to change it.

Most people struggle with this: we each create our own reality. Many believe that we have no choice but to live our destiny. Others believe that life is purely random, with luck and chance thrown in. Some religions suggest that our life is all the will of God, or Allah; some say that all our life is spent paying off karma. Some cynics and sceptics take a more humorous approach, having decided that everything in life has to be scientifically proven!

As an immortal Being, you are in a 3-dimensional reality to learn the laws of creation. Creating your every moment, and living the long-term reality that you create, is a very effective method of learning these inviolate laws.

The same laws are in action when you constantly and consciously . . . choose Love!

Collectively, humanity sleeps. Awakening is a choice that has to be acted upon.

A story is told about when God was walking the planet. Calling humanity together, God told them the latest cosmic-net joke. It went on and on. After six months nearly all of humanity was sound asleep. A year passed, and God reached the punch line, but nobody laughed. All humanity was asleep.

God smiled. "I forgot about linear time! Never mind, when you wake up, you'll get the joke."

When I awakened, I spent three days laughing, essentially because I was the joke. As you are!

Seriously, humanity went to sleep collectively.

Awakening is an individual one-by-one affair. It is a choice that you are required to make, and live, for only by living it can you pierce the dream of illusion we call life. To awaken, you need to be conscious. A powerful method to awaken is to constantly and consciously . . . choose Love!

November 15th

True prosperity begins with your awareness and appreciation of self/Self. True prosperity is not just about money, it is a measure of your overall relationship with life.

Most people think that prosperity is all about money, while it actually means to thrive, to do well, to flourish, and to have good fortune.

Money can buy most material things, but it cannot buy you a meaningful relationship, or true joy, or Love, or even perfect health if you lose it. In fact, many people spend their health in gaining their wealth.

Learn to appreciate yourself, and those whom you Love fully. Never take them for granted.

When you have an honouring relationship with yourself and the people in your life, so you will attract all levels of true prosperity. Remember, appreciation is fundamental to true prosperity.

As also is consciously . . . choosing Love!

Remember, what we give to other people we give to ourselves.

Be careful what you give to people. If you give them the distress of harsh words, you give discord to yourself. If you generate anger and impatience in other people, most of it will come and stay with you. Even if you think badly of others, it is your life that will reflect your thoughts and feelings.

Never get caught in the illusion that all life works out in a single lifetime. A lifetime is but one frame in the vast movie of Self. What goes out today will inevitably return on one of your tomorrows. What goes around, comes around!

Practice being loving, tolerant and accepting; all are positive and life supportive expressions.

As is consciously . . . choosing Love!

November 17th

Consciousness is the reality of life. Life is infinite in its expression. Life cannot be killed, nor can consciousness be extinguished.

Consciousness draws to itself physical form through which to express; the expression is consciousness. The death of physical form is simply that. Consciousness will continue undeterred. We are creative and intelligent expressions of consciousness. Are we? Hmm!

A species does not end simply because of the withdrawal of consciousness. The metaphysical form continues in a time frame that we do not occupy. Yet we regard this as the extinction of a species. Us . . . intelligent, hmm!

Viewing life through a single lifetime frame will reinforce strongly the illusions that ensnare us.

Pierce the illusions of life by constantly and consciously . . . choosing Love!

As you focus on Truth and live it, in perfect timing your metaphysical-Self will move into ascendancy in your life.

When you dwell in Truth, empowering it in your life by living it, a shift in consciousness takes place. A shift in you!

I vividly remember this happening to me. I knew instantly that there was no way back to the life of illusion and make believe that is now so very predominant in humanity.

You are, first and foremost, a metaphysical Being. Illusion may suggest that if so few people recognise this, therefore it is wrong.

History indicates that all too often Truth has resided in the awareness of the few.

Believe me, Truth in humanity is a minority movement!

You are in that movement while you always consciously . . . choose Love!

November 19th

The individual is the Whole – All that Is – the Whole is also the individual. This is Oneness.

When I write 'individual', this is exactly what I mean. Individuality is not the identity. The person with a name believing that this is who they are, is the personal-identity experience.

Look at it in a very different way. Individuality = in-divided-duality. The division is simply this: the physical mortal-self and the metaphysical immortal-Self. We focus on the physical only.

Holistically, I have removed the 'divide' out of my life, so that I seamlessly live the physical mortal and the metaphysical immortal, as One.

Any person who experiences identity-self as One with their greater-Self, moves toward this.

In any process of ascendency, a path is created by consciously . . . choosing Love!

Despite our infinite potential, most people focus only on a finite reality. This denies our greatest potential, for we 'are' Beings of infinity.

Walking your spiritual path requires you to develop a wider vision and a greater view of life. It requires you to be open and aware.

If you live this way, invariably you will get in touch with your infinite potential.

Discovering this infinite potential is exciting. You begin to realise that a greater reality exists, superimposing upon and beyond the images of illusion.

The more you live and express your infinite potential, so, gradually, this greater reality will reveal itself to you.

A greater reality is revealed when you always remember to consciously . . . choose Love!

NOVEMBER 21st

The past and future are no more than different frames in the greater reality of Now – this infinite moment.

In these pages I have repeatedly and deliberately drawn your attention to a far greater, timeless reality. This book is not designed to reinforce the illusions, but to encourage you to go well beyond them. This takes courage, and it is your courage that is of value, and is to your credit.

In my Intensives I show participants how time is not quite the way that it appears.

If – knowing it is linear time that enforces so much of the illusion – you find it possible to live in our linear time frame while developing a deeper relationship with your immortal-Self, then you are progressing steadily along the spiritual path of Truth.

You will maintain this progress with the daily practice of consciously . . . choosing Love!

As we change in the Now moment, both as the human race and individually, so we are altering continually the future and the past.

The less aware you are in your daily life, of your metaphysical-Self, and of living more consciously, the deeper your life will continue along the deep groove of habitual conformity.

The more aware you are of yourself, of your greater potential, and of consciously being in the moment, the more dramatic will be the changes in both your past and future.

The future and the past occupy the moment of Now. The more you truly experience the eternal moment, the more enriched your holistic reality becomes.

As it is for one person, so it is for whole nations. You positively change your future and your past by consciously choosing . . . Love, Now!

November 23rd

You cannot change and remain the same.

In my experience, just about everyone I meet wants to change *and* remain the same. Although generally unaware of it, those people who want change, cling to their destructive old habits with incredible tenacity. We invite change into our lives, and then fight either to reject it, or to fearfully avoid it. We need change to grow!

Change is the fresh wind of new potential and new opportunities. It is not out to hurt you, although change will ruthlessly destroy all that is no longer appropriate in your life.

You have to learn to release stuff, not cling! It is far less painful to invite change to work *with you*, rather than *against you.*

Painless change is created by constantly and consciously . . . choosing Love!

For most people, it is much easier to remain with what is utterly familiar through endless repetition, than it is risk the threat of change. Yet, endless repetition is by far the most painful to endure, by far the greatest risk.

If there is a threat to humanity, it is that of 'more of the same' – conformity! In the guise of stability, conformity encourages stagnation. In the guise of our security, sameness nourishes deep insecurity.

The mind likes uniformity, so people play the conformity game. Oh, the settings change from one century to another, but the same game of conformity will continue into oblivion – if we let it.

Embrace the changes in your life. Learn to let go of whatever it is that change is attempting to remove. Only fear holds on.

Create change for yourself by constantly and consciously . . . choosing Love!

NOVEMBER 25th

True change is the magic of pure alchemy. Controlled change is deception in the guise of modification. Modification is not change.

A woman looks in a mirror, and thinking to make a few changes, carefully applies a fair amount of cosmetics. The effect is just what she wants, so she is happy.

Despite this, her face remains completely unchanged. She modified the appearance of her face, but she did not change it. With cosmetic surgery, the structure of the face can be altered, but unless the unseen magical alchemy of change takes place in the consciousness of the person involved, then, apart from the illusion of appearance, nothing has truly changed.

Change is a force that frightens most people. More frightening by far is 'more of the same' that never ending conformity of decay.

Welcome change, even invite and embrace it. You do this by consciously . . . choosing Love!

Pain and suffering are a measure of your resistance to change.

My spiritual path was all pain and suffering. I do not recommend it. When pain is our teacher, we become accustomed to applying more pain so that we can learn our lessons.

I have no hesitation is stating that pain and suffering, in all its many endless ways, is by far the greatest addiction in humanity.

Because for so long we have feared the 'unknown' factor associated with change, we have developed a subconscious resistance to change. Yet change is programmed into life, for it is essentially growth and expansion.

We now associate change with suffering. In Truth, most of our stress and suffering is caused by our fearful resistance to change.

Invite and embrace change by constantly and consciously . . . choosing Love!

November 27th

Free will means that to use will freely your will must be aligned with Love.

People talk about free will as though it is a normal fact that we have free will – when it is actually a casualty of the way we live.

Thoughts of worry are not free will. Low self-esteem is not the result of free will, nor is anxiety, or stress, or depression.

People who are indoctrinated by their beliefs or religion do not have free will, nor do people with anger, blame, and fear. There is no free will in any emotional attachments whatsoever.

Free will is not thriving.

When your heart is filled with Love for yourself and all humanity, uncluttered by the illusions that beset your everyday reality, then your will is free to create and express lovingly.

Inner freedom is born when you consciously and freely choose to . . . choose Love!

Instead of thinking attack thoughts, think support thoughts.

So easy. So simple. So powerful. So life transforming. Yet . . . so rare!

The world is filled with troubled people. I often feel I am on the wrong planet, with a mind so peaceful, so uncluttered, so calm.

But . . . I remember. I remember when just the idea of support thoughts, instead of my usual attack thoughts, was a revelation.

You do not have to be a chaotic thinker at the mercy of your thoughts. You can choose the thoughts that you want: thoughts that honour you, thoughts that support you, and most importantly, thoughts that are based in an abiding Love toward yourself.

You can do this . . . if you think you can!

Toward yourself, always . . . choose Love!

NOVEMBER 29th

No matter what your thoughts are concerning your body, body-consciousness is ceaselessly acting upon those thoughts.

When you look in the mirror do you like what you see? Do you think, "I really Love this body of mine," or are your thoughts more judgemental and critical?

Every criticism of your body is received by the trillions of cells in your body, and they act on this. You will grow 'toward' all that you criticise, simply because this is your focus.

Similarly, if you look in the mirror feeling a glow of pride and happiness with your body, this will translate into good health and an overall feeling of well-being.

All I am saying here is that your body and you are One. Focussed thought has a very powerful effect, either for better, or worse.

It's up to you! Simply . . . choose Love!

What we think affects the choices of what
we eat. What we eat has a definite effect
on what we think.

If you are stressed and unhappy, you will have
stressed and unhappy thoughts. You cannot have
one without the other. This, in turn will create an
appetite for sweet and fatty foods . . . commonly
known as junk food.

These are the foods which create the bodily
conditions that will maintain stressed and deeply
worried thinking. Nasty cycle!

I am not about to advise you on your diet. Suffice it
to say that food which best supports and nourishes
your body, maintaining your required mineral,
fibre, nutrient and protein balance, is the food
that will most strongly sustain your thoughts of
high self-esteem, along with physical, mental, and
emotional well-being. Truly, this is life worth living.

All this fits hand in hand with constantly and
consciously . . . choosing Love!

The thirty-one days of the month of

December

Thought for the month:

*Most people see life as outside themselves.
Yet, in Truth, what you see is a reflection of
the inner state of your own life.*

*When you see an angry, negative world, it is
because you have anger and negativity within
yourself.*

*Better to realise that you are the aperture through
which life flows – that you are the very matrix in
the creation of your life, and that there is nothing
outside Self.*

Reflect on this!

December 1st

Honest, caring, open communication is the lifeblood of all relationships.

Swans pair for life. I once watched a pair of black swans on a small lagoon as they swam away on their respective forays for food, yet always coming back to each other with obvious affection. Beaks clicking, they would twine their necks together, reinforcing the life-bond to which they were committed. A more powerful communication I could not imagine.

I watched a person I know come home from work to where his wife was waiting. He just glanced at her, asked for a cup of tea, and slumped down in his chair to watch TV. As might be expected, the marriage eventually collapsed . . . and he was surprised!

Communication is communion, one person with another. It is called caring and sharing!

Please, for any relationship to work for each other, always consciously . . . choose Love!

Today, most men are no longer warriors,
they are worriers.

The number of male suicides in the Western
world attests to the stressed state of mind of
millions of men. Many men still carry an inner
program stating that they alone are responsible for
wife or partner and children.

Although intellect knows that it is now a shared
responsibility, especially in the financial area, the
sub-emotional program still continues.

The result is escalating stress and worry. First and
foremost, men, put down the battleaxe. Realise
that life is not a fight to be won. Indeed, you do not
have any opponents, except, all too often, yourself.

Communicate honestly with your wife, or partner.
Share with them just what it is that causes you so
much stress. Dare to be vulnerable.

A powerful way to de-stress is by constantly and
consciously . . . choosing Love!

December 3rd

Being friends with those whom you Love is far superior than your need to be right.

When my two eldest boys were about ten and twelve, we had a disagreement about something. That night, when I went to kiss them, they both turned their heads away. Give it time, I thought, because I'm right. The next night I got the same treatment, and the night following.

This was getting serious. As I thought about the issue, and of being right, I realised that the price of my being right was more than I was prepared to pay. I decided that being friends with my two boys was far more valuable to me than being right. I apologised to them the following night, and told them that they were right. We shared our heart-needed hugs and kisses. Such adult foolishness is all too common.

The way out is to let go of the need to be right, and always . . . choose Love!

Reduce your need to blame. Increase your ability to appreciate.

S eems simple enough! Yet, people mostly go into 'automatic blame' at the slightest incursion upon their perceived rights. This indicates that people who blame others automatically, also automatically blame themselves.

In other words, while you have a critical self-blame relationship with yourself, this negative cycle will continue.

Again, it begins with you and yourself. When you find the way to appreciate yourself naturally, you will naturally appreciate the other people in your life.

As always, this attracts ever more people and situations to appreciate.

The greatest stimulant for self-appreciation comes from consciously . . . choosing Love!

December 5th

You cannot be truly powerful, and also be one of the masses.

Blame takes away your power. Worry takes away your power. Anxiety takes away your power. Anger takes away your power.

Criticism takes away your power. Cynicism and scepticism take away your power. All drugs take away your power. Impatience takes away your power. Negative thinking takes away your power. Enough!

Unfortunately, all the above, plus far more, are common in the mass of humanity. It is these negative expressions that take the power from the vast majority of people.

For you to be truly powerful, these negative aspects of your everyday expression of self must all be released. Let them go.

This does not 'give' you power; it reveals the inherent power that is already within you.

You release your inner power when you first and foremost . . . choose Love!

*If you are in conflict with Self, then you are
in conflict with life.*

You cannot have outer conflict without inner
conflict, and inner conflict always comes
first. If you are a person who seems to be battling
continually to make life work for you, please be
aware that it is yourself against whom you are
really fighting.

The main reasons so many Australians love a
battler is simply because they so easily identify
with battling. They find it more difficult to identity
themselves with triumph.

Once again, it goes back to a simple Principle:
There is nothing outside Self. There is a whole lot
outside the identity and the body, but nothing
outside Self. Make friends with Self, and all
the inner and outer conflict is finally and fully
resolved.

It becomes obvious that again, for yourself, you
need to consciously . . . choose Love!

DECEMBER 7th

*To know the Truth of death, you have only
to learn the Truth of life.*

The Truth of death is very easy, simply because it
is not a reality. We are told that no one has died
and come back to talk about it. In Truth, everyone
continues to incarnate back, without their memory
of it.

For you, life is the growth and continuity of the
soul you are. For you, you are the full meaning of
life. The way you live either gives it more value and
meaning, or less.

In Truth, your life can have no more or less
meaning than it already has, but the way that
you conduct yourself in your daily life will either
reveal and express your potential, or it will remain
concealed in illusion.

To give the greatest Truth and meaning to your
life is simple . . . but not easy. Can you rise to a
challenge? Daily, at every opportunity, at every
potential argument or conflict, at every personal
insult, or in the face of anger, take a deep breath
and consciously . . . choose Love!

You have a problem only when you believe you have a problem. If you become a problem solver, you will create problems to solve.

When I talk to a person at an Intensive who is struggling with a major problem in their life, I ask them about their relationship with the problem. Basically, they always identify themselves *with* the problem. They also claim ownership, saying, "It is *my* problem." This is a very close, self-created relationship with a problem!

The Truth is, you are *not* the problem. You are a magnificent Being of Love and Light. If you develop a close relationship with this Truth, and talk of the problem as *a* problem, instead of *my* problem, you will find the resolution much easier, simply because you are no longer attaching yourself to the problem.

Most problems dissolve easily, and even better, do not appear, when you make the conscious choice to constantly . . . choose Love!

Desperation opens doorways, complacency closes them.

A person who reaches the place of desperation is a person on the brink of dynamic action. If you choose the negatives of desperation, then life is going to be a battlefield for you.

If, however, you choose the positives within your desperation, you will be empowered to make the choices, or act on choices that you were previously unable to do. This opens doorways into new potential.

Complacency is an attitude that rapidly evolves into a condition. Fundamentally, complacency means self-gratification and self-satisfaction.

There is nothing wrong with this, but when complacency overlooks the fact that life is a continuous unfolding of potential, you get easily lost in a stagnation of smugness.

Better by far to nurture the potential of your life by continuing the practice of . . . choosing Love!

*Our mission in life is to make ourselves more
of what we are, and less of what we are not.*

If you take this as *your* mission in life, it will take
you toward the nobility of Self. For you to become
less of what you are not, needs us to define
precisely what this means.

You are not separate from any other life-form.
You are not unworthy, or undeserving. You are not
naturally negative. You are not a Being of violence
or anger. You are not a person who is capable of
achievement only through struggle.

To make yourself more of what you 'are' is very
clear. You are a magnificent, metaphysical,
multidimensional immortal Being of Love and
Light.

You are worthy, and deserving of the best. You
are Love made physically visible in human form.
However, for this mission to be actualised, you *do*
have to live in a manner that is supportive to the
Truth of Self.

The most supportive manner that is humanly
possible is to consciously . . . choose Love!

December 11th

Small positive triggers can deliver great rewards.

Positive triggers are a form of catching your own attention when it begins to drift.

For example, you can have a few key words which on use, or when heard, bring you back to the moment, the people around you, and both yours and their needs.

If your loved ones thrive on appreciation, then find the words that trigger the greatest Love response. If you have children, parents, friends, each of them will have a particular word or phrase to which they respond positively and happily. "I Love you" is a very good way to go!

The more people you affect in this positive way, the more favourable impact there will be in your own life. Love wins, no matter what!

It is positive and uplifting for yourself and your family when you consciously . . . choose Love!

Reaction and repetition are lovers; from their alliance comes habit and sameness.

Many humans are very ritualistic. A lot of people like repetition, being automatically drawn toward it. When I begin a Intensive, and the participants are all seated, I know with a certainty, that unless I say otherwise, 99% of the people will go back to the same chair after every break, for the whole five-day duration of the Intensive. For each participant it quickly becomes 'my' chair!

Of course, I insist that the participants change chairs at every break, knowing that to some degree it will shatter their comfort zones of mindless repetition.

Try breaking some of the useless, repetitive patterns that are restricting you. You cannot be a new person with old habits!

A good way to shatter old habits is to always consciously choose the newness of . . . Love!

DECEMBER 13th

Old programs get resolved if we 'respond' to life;
reaction reinforces them.

When we react to an adverse situation in life, we are usually coming from a negative aspect of ourselves. When we do this, we reinforce and re-imprint the negative aspect all over again, thus ensuring that another reaction to a similar situation is waiting to happen.

When we respond favourably to a situation, we are choosing the positive aspect of ourselves. In this way we are giving ourselves the greatest opportunity to solve the problem, and erase the old repetitive program.

By its very nature, adverse reaction negates positive choice. Favourable response is the way toward resolution.

Like, consciously . . . choosing Love!

We become our repetitive thoughts, we become our repetitive attitudes.

This is simply another way of stating what I have written about thoughts and attitude. Be aware of what you think. If you are the owner of thoughts of hostility to another person – including world leaders! – it is to you that life will be hostile. You will find that for every negative thought you have, it is you who will be immersed in that negativity.

It is the same with your attitude to life. I truly recommend that you develop a sense of respect for yourself and for other people.

In this way you become a respectful person, and, in turn, become respected. Equally, self-respect us to consciously . . . choose Love!

DECEMBER 15th

*Let go of your many wants. Want is the voice
of poverty. Look instead toward what you have,
for appreciation of what you have is the path of
abundance.*

Many people believe that desire is the way to
manifest their needs. This is not so! Desire is
based in wanting. While you feed your desires you
will create ever more wants to desire.

If, instead of feeding want and desire, you learn
to appreciate what you already have, feeling a
genuine gratitude, you are then empowering a
higher way of manifesting your needs.

Wants reinforce the feeling that you are
unsatisfied, so dissatisfaction is the unwitting
consequence.

A grateful appreciation for what you already have
feeds gratitude. Have and appreciation hold hands.
Soon, you will have more for which to be grateful.

Add to this, the inner growth of unconditional Love
that you are creating, and your life is abundant. So,
keep on consciously . . . choosing Love!

*Wisdom is the art of knowing your limits, but
not allowing them to limit you.*

I went to a young Ali Woods piano concert, and
listened as this remarkable woman, aged twenty-
two, played with such immense energy, incredible
skill, and sheer towering passion, that the hall was
hushed in awe.

She told us that from the age of six, she practised
eight hours a day, every day.

Her early piano teachers told her that she was too
small to be a concert pianist, and that she would
not be strong enough. The limits they set for her
were their limits. Ali never made them her own. As
I write this, at her young age she is considered one
of the worlds great concert pianists.

Be careful with the imposition of *your* limits. Never
allow other people to set them for you. Know your
own limits, but do not get attached to them.

Know that you can do anything on which you
focus, if you are prepared to give your 'all' to
achieve it.

To blast aside all your limits . . . choose Love!

December 17th

Truth always reveals its presence through the heart –
the seat of the soul.

In your life, Truth is constantly presenting to
you the opportunities and moments for you to
recognise Truth in your life!

If you are a brain oriented person, most of this will
elude your awareness, because you are looking at
life through an intellectual lens.

Truth will not so easily find you.

If you are a person who looks at life through the
lens of intelligence, unclouded by intellect, you will
be opening yourself to Truth.

Truth and you will more easily connect.

There are no rights and wrongs to life, but
there are most certainly the repercussions and
consequences of the way we choose to live.

No greater way of life exists than to constantly and
consciously . . . choose Love!

*Your life is made up, and fabricated, from the
substance of your focus. Energy, creation, and their
manifestation and expression flow to where, and on
what, you give your full attention.*

Recognise that life is energy in continuous
creation, manifestation, and expression. You
and I have to participate in this as we have no
other choice. Death does not end our eternal
participation; nothing ends it. So, we might as well
enjoy the Game of Life, and play it well.

This energy of life flows through us. We have no
choice but to create, and then experience what we
create . . . and create . . . and create!

Learn to be aware of your daily preoccupations.
If they become negative, move them toward the
positive as quickly as possible. Develop a new
attitude of gratitude for all that you 'have' in your
life. These are good choices to make manifest. Be
grateful also for your growing wisdom and ability
to consciously . . . choose Love!

DECEMBER 19th

Continuous self-criticism is one of the most negative and destructive forces that you can create and unleash against yourself.

Are you a perfectionist? If you are, you can be certain that you are a person who is heavily self-critical. This does not make you morally wrong, but it does mean that you have to live under the strain and pressure of this continuous self-criticism.

If a survey were to be taken of those suffering heart attacks, I have little doubt that the majority of these people are, or were, perfectionists to some degree.

Regular self-criticism generates destructive energy, all of which is directed against yourself. Because it has become part of the human consciousness, your self-criticism joins forces with all the self-criticism of all other critical people. This is a massive amount of negative energy which, attracted by you to you, is discharged within your daily life. Not a good idea!

Better by far to overdose on self-appreciation, and on a daily basis, to consciously . . . choose Love!

Concern is the positive of care, while worry is its negative counterpart.

Worry is probably the all-time most common direction of human thinking. It is negatively based, which does not necessarily mean bad, but neither is it constructive, or good.

Worry always looks at the very 'worst' of any situation, adding nothing of any value to the people involved. It just adds more negativity!

Concern for a person, or a situation, looks for the positive. Concern sees the best possibilities, the greatest chances, the most optimistic of outlooks. Concern empowers the people who are involved, and feeds them positivity.

Release negative worry. Instead develop an attitude of positive and optimistic concern. And include the daily ration of . . . choosing Love!

December 21st

*A focus on fighting sickness will create
sickness to fight.*

If you are a person with a sickness, or any disease,
quit fighting it. *You are the sickness!*

First and foremost you need to accept that this is
your creation, no matter how inadvertent.

It could stem from the past in your life-movie, or it
may be a current happening off inner discord.

Rather than dwelling on the disease, fighting it,
focus as powerfully as possible on 'good health'
and, in both your emotions and thoughts, move
toward it. Visualise yourself as you were when you
were at your most healthy. Recapture that 'feeling'
of vitality, especially the emotion of it.

Bring all this into your moment, and make this
healthy, more vital image your immediate and
ongoing focus. Not easy, but *you, the unhealthy*
needs to become *you, the healthy!*

This may feel difficult to achieve when you are
sick, but whatever disease you can create, you can
also dis-create. In essence, this means that for
yourself, consciously . . . choose Love!

*If you take back your power, your power
will take you forward.*

Too much of human thinking diminishes
the thinker, rather than strengthens them.
You truly need to empower yourself with your
thoughts, but they will need to be much more
selective and constructive than is normal.

Most people no longer sit on the throne of power in
their own lives. While we blame governments for
our personal troubles, while we criticise ourselves,
while we are angry with the state of the world, we
are the cause of the erosion of our own power.

We can take back our power by living a life of
choice, rather than regurgitating the old sad
programs of our past; with positive choices we
move forward powerfully and progressively.

We also take back our power by constantly and
consciously . . . choosing Love!

December 23rd

It takes much intelligence to live a truly simple life, but only a little cleverness is required to live with complication and foolishness.

In a holistic world, intelligence and intellect are leagues apart. While it is quite possible to be highly intellectual and intelligent, it is rare. This is the truly gifted person.

Generally, intellect and complicity go hand in hand. So many clever people live their lives bouncing from one emotional trauma to the next, or from one financial crisis to the next. Of course, none of it is their doing, it is all somebody's fault, or just a run of bad luck!

When you live life intelligently, you appreciate the wisdom of the old saying, 'The greatest truths are the most simple.' To live with deep trust and openness is intelligent, just as it is to constantly and consciously . . . choose Love!

It is our insecurity that resists abundance.

Another paradox! Logical thinking would assume that insecurity screams out for affluence, but the opposite is true. It is very easy to teach a reasonably secure, or confident person how to attract abundance, but with the truly insecure – and they are the many – it is rather difficult.

Insecurity thrives on negative attention. Insecurity thrives on fear thoughts, on all the dread and self-punishment that accompanies it.

Consider insecurity as a nasty parasite feeding on its host. The longer it thrives, the stronger it becomes, and the more difficult it is to dislodge from the psyche of the host person.

You get rid of insecurity by empowering your sense of self. Things like self-appreciation, trust, self-respect, all lead toward security in yourself.

It is impossible to have self-Love and insecurity. So it helps greatly to always . . . choose Love!

December 25th

It is ironic that humanity can find only a single day in the year for celebrating goodwill and peace on Earth.

C hristmas Day is one of my favourite days of the year. In most of the Western world, we all make an effort to be loving and peaceful, all exchanging gifts. How absolutely marvellous!

But why only one day a year? Why not have one day a year really condemning and cursing governments, prime ministers, world leaders, nasty relatives, and everybody with whom you have a grudge? Why not get it all out of our system in one massive purging?

We could then go back to another three hundred and sixty-four days of Good Will to All and Peace on Earth?

Okay, I can dream! Have a very Happy Christmas. And remember, today especially, consciously and joyfully . . . choose Love!

The inner program that is most difficult to remove is the program that tells you how you think you should be.

We are all programmed to some degree. The formative years of our childhood are all about being programmed. Later, we spend much of our adult life either changing, or, more often, modifying the less desirable aspects of those earlier imprints.

Unfortunately, we then create a program which we think is better – a program of how we think that we should be. This is usually based in a critical self-analysis, looking at ourselves and our lives rather harshly, or in trying to conform with what is acceptable within our peer group.

Abandon all ideas and concepts of how you think you should be, and gracefully accept being who you are, and Loving who you are, just the way you are, right now! Of course, it always helps to consciously . . . choose Love!

December 27th

The more people you allow to go in front of you, the further ahead you will get.

Stop externalising life and view things from an holistic viewpoint. People are in a hurry these days, all trying to go 'somewhere' fast.

There are many people who do the rounds of New Age speakers, simply so they can include "I heard Michael Roads" in their conversation! Mind you, if this pleases them, then I would not deny them the inspirational kick.

Some are trying simply to keep in the front line of the latest New Age fashion, both in crystals, talks, looks and books.

Give it up. The more you focus on living Truth as you perceive and experience it, the more you are growing into the beautiful Being you truly are.

It matters not who is way out ahead of you in the continually changing trends of life, for you are always 'growing' ahead if you constantly and consciously . . . choose Love!

When you clean away the glaze of deception from the mirror of life, you get to see the clear, undistorted reflection of Truth.

We look into life through the distortion of illusion. Everything that appears so clear and so real is no more than illusion supported by our conditioned program of the past.

What humanity believes, and what we accept as everyday normality, is a very small part of what truly IS. One thing that we do *not* do collectively is perceive and experience a far higher and greater Truth.

To reach Truth is not a matter of *adding* a certain 'something' to your life; it is about *removing* from your life all the elements of negative distortions that make you and your life appear as so much less than is actually true. Consider once more the wisdom and clarity of consciously . . . choosing Love!

December 29th

A commitment to your spiritual path takes place only when you have the soul integrity that gives birth to it.

Just by being alive in this cycle of humanity means you are on your spiritual path. Everyone is. That said however, there are great numbers of people who would disown the thought of even being vaguely spiritual.

When you commit yourself consciously to your spiritual path, it has to be a 'real' commitment.

Many people commit themselves to a marriage without any real intention of honouring this commitment, while to others it is a sacred trust.

You are on your spiritual path only when you are fully committed – but not attached – to being on the path.

A true spiritual commitment requires you to be fully centred in living the unfolding Truth of Self. It is about 'consciously' living with a spiritual intent.

There is no grasping, holding, or wanting: this is an attachment to an outcome, not a spiritual path. It is all about choosing and living . . . Love!

*It is not the heart that needs to be healed; it is the
many expressions of our subconscious fear of life that
need healing.*

The simple reality is that people do fear life in
varying degrees. It is a program that has been
developed over millennia, and is now so deeply
buried, so horribly subtle, and so insidious, that we
live with a self-destruct agenda made even more
deadly by its ability to self-deceive.

Our heart is the area of the body most directly
affected by this. We suffer heart attacks, never
realising that it is self under attack, while the
heart – the seat of the soul – is the battleground
While a physical operation may sometimes repair
the physical damage, it mostly leaves the cause
untouched.

Only a deep commitment to Self and Truth can
operate in a way that removes the roots of self-
deceit and inherent fear.

To heal your heart, consciously . . . choose Love!

December 31st

It is said that when one door closes, another opens.
In Truth, one door closing allows you the opportunity
to open another door of your choice.

Generally, one door closing in life is a mini-ending. Right now a year in your life is about to close. You stand on the brink of a whole new potential, a new opportunity.

What will you do? Will the next year be an almost exact repeat of this one, more of the same, or are you ready to open the doors of change as this year comes to a close?

Life is not about endings and beginnings, but it is about Change and Newness. During the year as you have read the pages of this book, hopefully you have learned about life as it truly is. Now you have a new opportunity. You have the perfect chance to let old habits finish, and new expressions of self/Self begin.

As the old year closes, you are being offered a unique opportunity for newness. If, under all negative and positive circumstances, you truly do see the wisdom of Love, then let this be your daily choice. You will never regret it.

A Few Last Words

I t will be obvious in these pages that I have pushed home my world-wide message of consciously ... choosing Love! I have done this deliberately, and without repentance! In all my years of spiritual counselling, I have learned that there is no such thing as a true/real human problem. I have learned that there is only a deep lack of self-Love. When I say lack of Love, I mean exactly this: a frightening and disturbing lack of Love for ourselves. It is widespread, common, and extremely self-negating and self-destructive.

This lack of self-Love manifests itself in endless and countless ways, and always we are the unwitting victims. Sadly, this lack of self-Love is all too often replaced with, at its worst, self-hate and self-loathing, moving up the scale to self indifference and the very common, not-good enough-self. The whole key to changing your life is in being conscious. This is why, over and over, I *consciously* write the word *consciously*.

Please get this ... you are Love made manifest.

You are worthy of the best that life can give you, but you have to *choose it and live it.* For the last time in these pages, let me assure you that you can change your whole life for the better – *wonderfully and magnificently better* – if, every day, in all your thoughts, your words, and in your every action, you constantly and consciously choose . . . unconditional Love!

In Love and Light . . . Michael J. Roads

www.ingramcontent.com/pod-product-compliance
Lightning Source LLC
Chambersburg PA
CBHW032032080426
42733CB00006B/60